INTERACTIVE STUDY GUIDE

VIDEO SESSIONS INCLUDE **MAX LUCADO** & HOSTED BY **MYRKA DELLANOS**

INTERACTIVE STUDY GUIDE

DR. ROBERT G. MARBUT JR.

transforming lives together

NO ADDRESS
Published by David C Cook
4050 Lee Vance Drive
Colorado Springs, CO 80918 U.S.A.

Integrity Music Limited, a Division of David C Cook
Brighton, East Sussex BN1 2RE, England

DAVID C COOK® and related marks are registered trademarks of David C Cook.

ISBN 978-0-8307-8729-6
eISBN 978-0-8307-8730-2

Cover Design: The Marketing House
Cover Photo: MP Studio – stock.adobe.com

Printed in the United States of America
First Edition 2024

1 2 3 4 5 6 7 8 9 10

120723

We dedicate this interactive study guide to all the people experiencing homelessness and their families, and to the volunteers, staffers, and organizations that are trying to reduce homelessness across the US.

Contents

Acknowledgments

A very diverse group of individuals and organizations from all over the United States have come together to help unify the vision of reducing the homelessness crisis across America, starting with simply doing a better job of what we are doing now.

I am so thankful they have joined the *No Address* movement and are embarking with me on a journey to meaningfully address the unhoused in our country.

The *No Address Interactive Study Guide* is the start of our journey.

I thank Dr. Robert G. Marbut Jr. for inspiring and leading the effort to create this guide for use by groups within the faith and non-profit communities. Without him, there would be no interactive study guide.

He has assembled an outstanding team of national experts and leaders from the faith-based and non-profit communities to be contributors to the individual sessions within this guide. We are so thankful for all our editorial content contributors who have shared their wisdom: Dr. Denis G. Antoine II, John Ashmen, Rev. Ron Brown, Barbara Duffield, Rev. Robert Gehman, Commissioner Jolene Hodder, Dr. Roxanne Jordan, Dr. Robert G. Marbut Jr., Rev. John Samaan, and Rev. Brandan Thomas.

The whole team wants to recognize Andrea Lucado Ramsay, who edited and significantly improved our prose while thoughtfully structuring the overall study guide. A big thanks to Layne Pittman, who powerfully organized and edited all the supporting video segments within each session, and to Stephen Wollwerth, who provided segments and transcriptions from the *Americans with No Address* documentary. An enormous thank-you to Myrka Dellanos for hosting the videos, and to Greg Lucid for providing the music. A very special thank-you to Kenny

Wilson, Steve Green, and Max Lucado, who have supported and improved this guide at multiple points during the project.

A special thanks goes to Rebekah Hubbell, who has promoted this project from the beginning and for connecting Dr. Marbut and myself with the world-class David C Cook publishing team. She also worked with Dr. Marbut on developing the initial structure of this study guide.

The David C Cook publishing team has been amazing. They have organized and molded the writings of ten amazing authors into a powerful book. Thank you to the whole David C Cook team, especially Chadd Miller, Michael Covington, Stephanie Bennett, Caroline Cilento, Rudy Kish, Jack Campbell, Justin Claypool, James Hershberger, and Susan Murdock.

No Address—The Big 5!

This study guide has four companion products under the Robert Craig Films umbrella, when including the study guide, we call it The Big 5! ... The movie *No Address*, the documentary *Americans with No Address*, the *Interactive Study Guide*, the novel *No Address,* and the music album.

I am so thankful to my fellow producers of our *Americans with No Address* documentary and the *No Address* theatrical movie: Angela Lujan, Sally Forcier, Dr. Robert G. Marbut Jr., Philip Mangano, Julia Verdin, Nikki Vogt, Ashanti, Jennifer Stolo, Lucas Jade Zumann, Tina Douglas, and Stephan Dweck Esq. A big thanks to *New York Times* bestselling author Ken Abraham, who is the writer of our captivating novel *No Address*.

Many of the actors involved in the *No Address* movie have also been involved in the *Americans with No Address* documentary, in particular ... Ashanti, William Baldwin, Xander Berkeley, Ty Pennington, Lucas Jade Zumann, Isabella Ferreira, Patricia Velasquez, and Marbella Avilez.

Robert Craig Films

And a tremendous thanks to the Robert Craig Films team as well as the Robert Craig Films Foundation non-profit, who have kept all the trains running on time and coordinated the production efforts of the entire Big 5: Jennifer Stolo, Angela Lujan, Nikki Vogt, and Christie O'Malior.

Our Families

None of this would be possible without the support of our families. Many of whom have directly pitched in to help develop The Big 5 products. They have all put up with our crazy work hours, late-night Zooms, and weekend phone calls.

I am so thankful to my family, who has supported me in the creation and development of Robert Craig Films and our social impact productions on the homeless crisis. God has truly blessed me with thirty-two years of wonderful marriage with my wife, Natascha Lenney, who has been by my side throughout this journey. We have two fabulous children, who give us so much joy: our son, Jordan Lenney, and our daughter, Shiloh Lenney. I would also like to give a very special thanks to Meghan Duffey, who is a wonderful inspiration to me and such a blessing to the family.

I would like to give a big shout-out to my mom and dad, Dee Dee and Bob Lenney, who have been such a support throughout all these productions of The Big 5. I can't forget Natascha's mom either, Gordana Roessler, who has such a big heart for those experiencing homelessness and is always asking me, "Is there anything I can do?"

I also want to thank the spouses of the extended Robert Craig Films family, who have each been directly involved with the *No Address* projects: Keith Diederich, Johnny Lujan, and David Vogt.

My Lord and Savior

Most important, I believe God has a plan for us to make quality films with spiritually uplifting stories. It is important that our movies are filled with inspiration and hope, films that make people smile, that bring a high level of entertainment for the audience. We want everything that we produce to honor God and His Son, Jesus Christ.

Robert Craig

Introduction

When I was engaged with the White House working for the President of the United States (appointed by President Trump, with a short carryover into the Biden Administration) and the leaders of Congress as the Executive Director of the US Interagency Council on Homelessness (often referred to as the "Federal Homelessness Czar"), I was often asked by pastors, priests, youth directors, chairs of mission committees, and other faith leaders what their congregations could do to help address the homelessness crisis in our communities.

The faith community has a long history of providing a beacon of hope for people experiencing homelessness. The Salvation Army and some of the Citygate Network rescue missions (formally known as the Association of Gospel Rescue Missions) date back to the 1860s and 1870s. It was faith groups who took the lead in responding to homelessness from the ramifications of the Civil War, through the economic hardships of the Great Depression, to the recent uncertainties of the Great Recession and the COVID-19 pandemic, and all the decades in between.

In many ways the government is a late comer to addressing homelessness, only taking up the issue in an official capacity in 1987. That is when Congress passed the McKinney-Vento Homeless Assistance Act, and President Reagan signed it into law, which formally tasked many federal departments and agencies to work on homelessness issues.

Homelessness has been increasing dramatically in the United States since 2013. This is long before COVID-19, which some mistakenly assume caused a rise in homelessness. For the last decade, the numbers of families with children and adults experiencing homelessness have been skyrocketing in many parts of the United States, with many communities in crisis and some officially declaring states of emergencies. Nationwide, the issue of homelessness has become the number one or two local political issue in most medium and large cities. The challenges of homelessness are no longer isolated to our inner cities. Recently, many suburban and rural communities are starting to see dramatic increases in homelessness as well.

According to the US Department of Education (ED), there are almost 1.5 million children experiencing some type of homelessness within all five ED homelessness categories, while the US Department of Housing and Urban Development (HUD) reports nearly 1.2 million adults experiencing homelessness within all five HUD homelessness categories (more on these in the following glossary section as well as session 1). Taken together, almost 3 million people are experiencing homelessness of some type, and most advocates think the number is significantly higher.[1]

Homelessness has become a crisis because most people—including many governmental officials—fail to understand the interlocking issues of homelessness, untreated mental illness, and addiction, as well as PTSD, domestic violence, and sex trafficking. It is impossible to honestly address and solve homelessness if we do not take into consideration the real root causes of homelessness. That is the purpose for creating this resource guide: *to generate a more effective response to homelessness, especially within the community of faith and non-profit agencies, who have historically led the way in this endeavor.*

The *No Address Interactive Study Guide* team has assembled a diverse group of some of the smartest and most thoughtful faith-based public-policy advocates within the homelessness assistance community to create this resource. From the nationwide leaders of The Salvation Army USA and the Citygate Network to local operators of some of the most successful organizations around the nation, we investigate homelessness from all angles. Our contributors range from national policy leaders to local city hall advocates. We have subject-matter experts on families with children experiencing homelessness as well as experts on adult-level homelessness. You will also hear from people with "lived" homelessness experience, and individuals with family histories of homelessness. From pastors to lay leaders, this is a wonderful gathering of faith-oriented contributors who will lead us through the study of homelessness.

The *No Address Interactive Study Guide* starts with an overview of homelessness, including basic terminologies, important data, and key strategies. We then take a deep dive into the most important homelessness issues of the day, as well as debunk several myths about homelessness. We end with how congregations and individuals can help to dramatically reduce homelessness.

The journey you are embarking on will likely challenge your thinking about homelessness, and hopefully positively inform your personal response and your call to action. This effort will literally save lives, improve your community, and likely change you in the process.

Dr. Robert G. Marbut Jr.

Glossary of Key Homelessness Terms

As you go through this study, you may encounter some unfamiliar terms. Homelessness is a major issue, with multiple government agencies and non-profits devoted to addressing the issue. The staff and volunteers who work in this sector almost have their own language. Below is a list of some of the most used words and phrases in the field and what they mean in the context of homelessness. It is our hope that as you begin your own research and work with homelessness in your community, you will become more familiar with the language of homelessness, which will help you to be more comfortable working in this field, and reaching out to help and share your love.[1]

Affordable Housing – When individuals and families at or below the local median household income level can rent or buy housing. This can be a stand-alone house, condominium, or apartment. Affordable housing is often taxpayer-subsidized.

Annual Homelessness Assessment Report (AHAR) – An annual report requiring HUD to provide to Congress nationwide counts of homelessness. The number of people, mostly adults, experiencing homelessness is reported in five major categories based on the type of housing: Unsheltered, Emergency Shelters, Transitional Housing, Rapid Rehousing, and Permanent Supportive Housing.

Barriers to Housing – Challenges that act to prevent individuals and families from getting and maintaining housing. Examples include unemployment, criminal records, lack of identification, mental illness, and substance use disorders.

Behavioral Health – Refers to how behaviors impact an individual's well-being, and is distinct from mental illnesses. Substance use disorders, alcoholism, and gambling fall under the general umbrella of behavioral health.

Campuses – More robust versions of Transformational Centers, and are known for having extensive wraparound services provided by multiple partners working collaboratively at one site.

Chronic Homelessness – Living in a place not meant for human habitation for at least twelve months or four separate episodes of homelessness (one night or more not properly housed) in a three-year period.

Come-as-You-Are (CAYA) Facilities – Homelessness assistance centers, campuses, and shelters that accept everyone as they are as long as they are not a threat to themselves or others. Different from a "wet shelter" in that CAYA facilities do not allow on-site drinking and drug use.

Continuum of Care (CoC) – A quasi-governmental, self-appointed regional body organized to determine local funding allocations of housing subsidies for families and individuals experiencing homelessness.

Cooling or Warming Centers – Short-term intermittent facilities, generally open for eight to ten hours a day when "triggered" by extremely high or low temperatures.

Disability – A physical, intellectual, or developmental inability to do any substantial gainful activity that has lasted for a continuous period of twelve months or more. Chronic homelessness with a diagnosis of a substance use disorder is considered a disability and qualifies a person who is experiencing homelessness for Supplemental Security Income and Social Security Disability Income.

ED – Abbreviation for the US Department of Education, which is the lead funding agency for most federal programs that address families with children experiencing homelessness.

Emergency Shelter – A facility that provides temporary food and shelter for people experiencing homelessness.

Enabling vs. Engaging – Enabling is a dysfunctional activity, often by a well-intended person or group, that attempts to fix a problem but actually makes the problem worse by perpetuating and/or exacerbating the problem. Whereas, engaging is a positive activity that attracts or involves a person into treatment and onto a pathway to sustained recovery and/or self-sufficiency.

Encampments – Locations where two or more people experiencing homelessness live in an unsheltered area. Typically composed of tents and improvised structures, and can be in urban, suburban, or rural settings.

HEARTH Act of 2009 – The Homeless Emergency Assistance and Rapid Transition to Housing Act. A federal law that established the definition of chronic homelessness and authorized the Continuum of Care Program as the means to distribute federal grants to local communities for homelessness assistance.

Homelessness Assistance Centers, Navigation Centers, and Transformational Centers – A wide range of facilities and programs that have robust, wraparound trauma-informed services that focus on helping people to exit homelessness, with the ultimate goal of self-sufficiency. These centers are almost always open twenty-four hours a day, every day of the year. They are not "shelters."

Housing First – An approach that centers on trying to address homelessness by providing taxpayer-funded housing vouchers free of charge to people experiencing homelessness. Per HUD regulations and the Housing First philosophy, mandatory participation in treatment services is not allowed, and HUD funding for treatment services is not provided.

Housing Management Information System (HMIS) – A local information technology system used to collect data on the provision of housing and services to individuals and families experiencing homelessness.

Housing Unit – A house, apartment, or condominium intended for occupancy as a separate living quarter.

HUD – Abbreviation for the US Department of Housing and Urban Development, which is the lead funding agency for most federal programs that address adult homelessness.

Inclement Shelters – Short-term intermittent facilities generally open for ten to fourteen hours at a time when "triggered" by extreme weather conditions, such as exceedingly high temperatures (105 degrees or higher), very low temperatures (39 degrees or lower), tornados, floods, hurricanes, etc.

Intensive Case Management – A program for people experiencing homelessness—who often have severe and persistent mental illness and/or substance use disorder issues—that includes services like medication management, mental health wellness classes, substance use disorder treatment, twelve-step programs, help getting and keeping a job, etc.

Long-Term Supportive Care – Includes housing and customized supportive services, mostly for individuals receiving Supplemental Security Income, Social Security Disability Insurance, Medicare, and Medicaid.

Martin v. Boise (2018) – Currently the most important federal court case regarding homelessness as it relates to local governmental powers to address homelessness. The court ruled in *Martin v. Boise* that cities cannot enforce anti-camping ordinances if they do not have enough homeless shelter beds available as an alternative. Even though this case is in the Ninth Judicial Circuit, the US Supreme Court "let stand" this Ninth Judicial Circuit opinion; therefore, many federal district judges within other circuits use *Martin v. Boise* to guide their opinions. This case recently replaced *Pottinger v. Miami* as the most important court case regarding homelessness.

Master Case Management – A service provided by a homelessness assistance services provider that coordinates overall treatment for people experiencing homelessness across a variety of service providers.

McKinney-Vento Homeless Assistance Act of 1987 – The federal law that provides regulations and funding of many homelessness assistance programs. The act originally generated fifteen programs providing a spectrum of services to people experiencing homelessness, and created the United States Interagency Council on Homelessness, whose executive director is known as the "Federal Homelessness Czar."

Mental Health – Reflects emotional, psychological, and social well-being.

Mental Illness – Refers to conditions that negatively affect a person's thinking, feeling, mood, or behavior. These can include, but are not limited to, depression, anxiety, bipolar disorder, or schizophrenia.

Notice of Funding Availability/Notice of Funding Opportunity (NOFA/NOFO) – The public notice by the federal government of grants and other funding available to address homelessness issues. NOFAs/NOFOs define what eligible activities qualify for funding and how to apply for funds.

Outcomes vs. Outputs – Outcomes are the desired end goals to be accomplished (e.g., how many people exit homelessness). Outputs are sub-step actions that contribute toward accomplishing outcomes (e.g., how many hygiene kits are given out). When evaluating success, it is more important to measure and track meaningful outcomes than outputs.

Outreach Services – Services that attempt to engage and persuade people experiencing homelessness to go into a trauma-informed treatment program or to accept housing.

Permanent Supportive Housing – Leased-based taxpayer subsidized housing for people experiencing homelessness. Per HUD, participation treatment requirements and services are not allowed to be mandatory.

Point-in-Time Count (PITC) – A count of people experiencing homelessness (both unsheltered and sheltered) on a single day in January. This number is used by the federal government to track numbers and demographics of homelessness across the country. A PITC is required by HUD for communities that receive federal homelessness assistance funds and is one of the responsibilities of the local Continuum of Care.

Preconditions – Distinct from service participation requirements, these are used to prequalify individuals to participate in a program based on screening requirements. Preconditions and screening requirements could include sobriety, absence of a serious mental illness, or ability to work.

Rapid Re-Housing (RRH) – An intervention that provides tenant-based rental assistance to households experiencing homelessness for up to twenty-four months. Per HUD and the Housing First philosophy, participation treatment requirements and services are not allowed to be mandatory.

Serious Mental Illness (SMI) – A mental or emotional disorder resulting in serious functional impairment, which substantially interferes with or limits one or more major life activities of daily living.

Service Participation Requirements – Included in government funded assistance programs, such as Pell Grants and Temporary Assistance for Needy Families (TANF), are activities a person must participate in to continue to receive taxpayer funded assistance. Activities may include attending meetings with case managers, job training, life skill classes, and participation in substance use disorder treatment. Per HUD regulations and the Housing First philosophy, it is illegal to make participation treatment requirements mandatory.

Services – A wide array of assistance activities provided by a service agency for people experiencing homelessness. May include, but are not limited to, trauma-informed care, case management, substance use disorder treatment, treatment for mental illness, dental care, health care, job skills training, life skill classes, laundry, and hygiene care.

Shelters – Provide minimal services and focus on basic life safety services like food and housing; sometimes open part-time. Shelters are not Homelessness Assistance Centers, Navigation Centers, or Transformational Centers.

Smart Love – Activities that simultaneously utilize the passions of the heart and the smarts of the brain to positively engage people who are experiencing homelessness by encouraging them to enter treatment and recovery programs, while not enabling bad habits.

Substance Use Disorder (SUD) – Clinically significant impairment due to alcohol and/or drug use and addiction, including health problems, disability, and failure to accomplish responsibilities at work, school, or home.

Summer and Winter Shelters – Shelters operating over a finite period of time, usually three to five months, depending on local weather conditions. These shelters are generally open ten to fourteen hours a day, but are sometimes open 24-7.

Transitional Housing (TH) – Housing provided with accompanying wraparound supportive services to individuals and families experiencing homelessness for up to twenty-four months.

Trauma-Informed Care – A customized approach of care that addresses an individual's underlying history of trauma.

Wet Shelters – Facilities that allow on-site drinking and sometimes on-site drug use.

Wraparound Services – A wraparound approach provides customized robust treatment services based on the unique individual needs of the person experiencing homelessness.

Myths about Homelessness

Myth #1: All homelessness is the same.
The truth: Homelessness cohorts vary widely.

The US Department of Education (ED) and the US Department of Housing and Urban Development (HUD) have different definitions and metrics of homelessness. ED focuses their work on families with children experiencing homelessness while HUD focuses on adults experiencing homelessness. HUD and ED each track five different sub-categories of homelessness, for a total of ten main homelessness cohorts with dozens of additional sub-categories. For example, a child living in a car with their mom is in a very different cohort from an adult male veteran experiencing PTSD living on the street. Therefore, when discussing and thinking about homelessness, it is always important to clearly know which cohort is being addressed, and to understand that the treatment needs to vary among the different cohorts.

Myth #2: Adult street-level homelessness is a hunger problem.
The truth: Street-level homelessness is a complex web of several issues and is most often caused by a combination of mental illness and substance abuse.

Almost every adult transformational center, navigation center, and campus provides nineteen to twenty-one nutritiously balanced meals per person every week, with many providing box lunches and dinners for daytime and nighttime workers, respectively. Handing out sandwiches and other food in parks or on the street is almost always an enabling activity that negatively discourages adults experiencing homelessness from entering treatment programs. Additionally, because of the lack of food safety training, there have been many cases of food poisoning on the street, and the food that is given out on the street is seldom part of a balanced nutritional program. Every agency providing homelessness services needs help in preparing and serving meals, especially on non-holidays. Instead of handing out food or cash on the street, it is better to come alongside an existing successful agency and help them to prepare and serve the meals within their programs.

Myth #3: To solve homelessness, all we have to do is arrest everyone experiencing homelessness.
The truth: We cannot arrest our way out of homelessness.

Many cities have tried to eliminate homelessness by arresting the people experiencing homelessness, but this has never worked for two reasons. First, judges and jails generally release people out of incarceration in just a few hours. And second, very seldom are targeted treatment services available in jails for people experiencing homelessness.

Myth #4: To solve homelessness, we need to give away tents, sleeping bags, and food, so people can camp in public.
The truth: Giving away camping supplies only enables homelessness.

Some organizations support and encourage people experiencing homelessness to stay in parks, wooded areas, and on the streets, saying it is their civil right to camp on someone else's property. But people do not recover on park benches. True recovery occurs within well-run treatment and recovery programs. We will only reduce homelessness if we engage people into thoughtfully designed trauma-informed programs.

Myth #5: People experiencing homelessness choose to become homeless.
The truth: People can get stuck in the cycle of homelessness, but they almost never choose it.

Of all the contributors to this project, not one of us knows of a person or family who chose to become homeless. Children in K–12 classrooms do not dream of one day being homeless. However, the contributors of this project do know of individuals who have become stuck in homelessness or of individuals whose situation is currently being enabled. We therefore need to do everything possible to engage people into a pathway to recovery.

Myth #6: Everyone experiencing homelessness is service and/or housing resistant.
The truth: Most people experiencing homelessness will accept help when it is thoughtfully offered to them.

Generally 70 to 85 percent of people experiencing homelessness will accept treatment and recovery services when service options are respectfully offered. It is therefore important to thoughtfully develop the right type and right quantity of trauma-informed services.

Myth #7: Helping people experiencing homelessness only enables homelessness. What we need is tough love.
The truth: Tough love is not a good motivator and does not work.

If we engage people experiencing homelessness with dignity and respect, if we help the homelessness community with *"smart love,"* and if we positively engage individuals rather than negatively enable people experiencing homelessness, we then can successfully help people receive the services and treatment they need to exit the condition of homelessness forever. Programs like The Salvation Army, Citygate Network Rescue Missions, and numerous independent organizations have decades-long histories of success (some with more than one hundred years of success). Come alongside a successful agency and observe how they love and engage people who are experiencing homelessness, and then support the existing agency with your time, talents, and treasure.

Myth #8: Panhandling is harmless, and giving cash out of my car window helps people experiencing homelessness.
The truth: Giving money directly to someone experiencing homelessness is almost always an enabling behavior and often funds addiction and prostitution.

Seldom does cash given out on the street go to food and housing; instead, it almost always goes to alcohol, drugs, and prostitution. It is important to remember that most formal programs that help people experiencing homelessness provide nineteen to twenty-one meals a week. A thoughtful way to help with your money is to make direct contributions to extraordinarily successful faith-based and non-profit service organizations. These groups can always use the help, and you will know that your giving will go toward positive activities.

How to Use This Study Guide

Welcome to the *No Address Interactive Study Guide*. The book you are holding is part of a series of resources created to raise awareness about homelessness, including the *Americans with No Address* documentary, the *No Address* feature film, and the novel *No Address*.

None of these materials are required for this study, but if you want to dig even deeper into the issue of homelessness, they are excellent resources. Visit www.NoAddressMovie.com for more information.

This interactive study guide features newly written material by leading national experts who were interviewed and captured on video. Through this study, you will learn about the state of homelessness in our nation today and come away equipped to do something about it, empowered by God's Word and the example that Jesus set in Scripture.

What to Expect

Most likely, you signed up to participate in this study with a group, though you can certainly do it as an individual (see the "Participating as an Individual" section on page 32 for more details). We hope your group time allows you to get to know others in your faith community who are interested in homelessness, as well as to encourage one another in your faith and inspire each other to action.

This study is made up of four sessions that can be completed over the course of four to six weeks if your group meets weekly. Each session includes the following.

Reading: Before each group meeting, you will have a reading based on that week's topic. These are short chapters written by some of the most prominent voices in the country who are working to reduce homelessness. It may be difficult to find opportunities to do the readings outside of your group time, but fitting them into your schedule is highly encouraged. Each contributor has a wealth of knowledge to offer, and doing the reading beforehand will ensure that your group has time for deeper discussion.

The opening readings are intended to be completed in advance of meeting, so here's a suggested plan:
Before session 1, read pages 37–57.
Before session 2, read pages 63–73.
Before session 3, read pages 79–90.
Before session 4, read pages 95–104.

Group discussion time: During your group time, your leader will present several questions or topics for discussion (based on the pre-read material, the video clips during your session, and the suggested Bible passages). These prompts are printed in your study guide so you can consider them in advance and be prepared to participate, but also be willing to go where the discussion leads.

Video: At the beginning and end of your group time, you will be prompted to watch an intro and wrap-up video for each session crafted from interviews with the *Americans with No Address* documentary experts and others. In addition to intro and wrap-up videos, session 1 includes an overview video (to be watched first) that will introduce the big picture of the *No Address* project and the companion products. These videos are supplementary to your reading and will give you a deeper glimpse into the work that's being done around the country to help those who are experiencing homelessness.

Note: All videos can be accessed via the QR code (and link) on page 36. Pause to watch the corresponding video from your phone or computer when prompted in each session.

Unique questions are provided for each video, but good starting questions for each session could be: What thoughts or feelings do you have after watching the interviews? Which parts resonated with you, and why?

"Go and do": You have read, watched, and discussed. Now it is time to go and do! This section is perhaps the most important part of your group time. In Luke 10, Jesus tells the parable of the Good Samaritan. When He finished telling the story, Jesus told the expert in the law to "go and do likewise" (Luke 10:37). That passage is what inspired this section. At the end of each group time, you and your group will determine an action item based on what you read and watched in that week's session.

Prayer time: At the end of each group meeting, you will have an opportunity to share prayer requests and spend time together in prayer. This will allow you to get to know your fellow participants better and to know how you can encourage them throughout the week.

Between Sessions

If you want to continue learning and studying throughout the week between your group sessions, we have provided two ways for you to do this in addition to each week's reading:

Additional resources: At the end of each session is a list of additional resources. These are books, articles, and videos that address various issues on homelessness. Choose one (or all) to engage in before your next session.

Reflect: This section allows you to journal or reflect on your "Go and Do" action items for the week. You can also use this space to write down any additional thoughts or prayers you have from that week's session.

Participating as an Individual

If you are participating in this study as an individual, you can do everything listed above. The only alteration would be to the group "Go and Do" item at the end of each session. We encourage you to connect with the resources listed in the study guide or get involved with a local organization that is working with the homelessness in your community so you can put into practice what you have learned.

If you liked the study, invite friends to join you and go through it a second time as their group leader or facilitator.

What to Bring to Group

For each session, you will need to bring a few materials:

- Your copy of the *No Address Interactive Study Guide*
- A Bible
- A computer, phone, or other device capable of streaming the videos
- A pen or something to write with
- An open heart and mind, ready to receive God's Word

Notes for Group Leaders

Thank you for being a leader for the *No Address Interactive Study Guide*. Your role is vital to making this study happen, but do not feel too much pressure. Everything you need is right here in this guide: discussion questions, written material, videos, and Scripture references. You simply need to facilitate an environment where your group feels welcome and safe to share their thoughts and explore God's Word.

If you do not already have a leader or facilitator for your group, select one before your first meeting. It is important to have one designated person to lead or facilitate discussion, organize meetings, send email updates, and help keep the study on track.

Before Your First Meeting

Before your group meets for session 1, send an email or reach out to your group members with the following information:

- How to purchase the *No Address Interactive Study Guide*. They will need to secure a copy at least one week before your group meets so they have time to do the reading for session 1.

- Reading details. Each session includes reading that should be completed before your group time. For session 1, read the chapters on pages 37–57.

- Time and place to meet. Ideally this will be the same each week, but determine what's best for your group.

- Information about the other resources available in the *No Address* collection. This includes the *Americans with No Address* documentary, the *No Address* feature film, and the novel *No Address*. Explain to your group members that they do not *have* to watch or read any of these materials. They are simply supplementary resources. The videos they will need to view are accessed for free through the QR code (or link) on page 36. See the following sections for more details.

How to Structure Your Group Time

Each session is structured to take about an hour for a group to work through. This will vary, of course, but it is wise to leave about an hour and a half for each group meeting to allow for chatting before and after group as well as extra time for discussion or prayer if needed. If you follow an approximately one-hour format, your active session time will look something like this:

| Welcome... 10 minutes | Watch Session Intro Video... 10 minutes (approximately) | Discussion... 25 minutes | Go and Do... 10 minutes | Watch Session Wrap-up Video... 5 minutes (approximately) | Pray... 5 minutes |

Videos

Each session consists of two videos, the Intro Video to be played at the beginning of your group time and the Wrap-up Video toward the end. (Session 1 includes a ten-minute overview video as well.) If possible, have these videos queued up and ready to be played before the session begins. You can access the videos via the QR code (or link) on page 36, which takes you to a landing page for *No Address*. Once on the site, the videos are organized by session, so they're easy to find. You can play the video on a computer or share it on a larger screen, whatever works best for your group.

Our host for the *No Address Interactive Study Guide* videos is humanitarian, journalist, and television and radio host Myrka Dellanos. The videos for each session feature talks with our experts, and you will also hear from a variety of other respected voices who are dedicated to the mission.

Group Discussion Dynamics

When facilitating group discussion, anything can happen. You might have a quiet group that struggles with conversation. Or you might have the opposite: a dynamic group that easily gets off track. Regardless, group discussion time can be fruitful for building relationships, encouraging each other spiritually, and inspiring one another to see homelessness in a new and productive way. Keep the following tips in mind as you lead your group through the discussion portion of each session.

- **Do not be afraid of silence.** If you pose a question and no one answers right away, do not panic, and do not rush to fill the silence. Trust that someone will speak up when he or she is ready. You can even use the "seven-second rule." After asking a question, count to seven in your head. If no one speaks up before then, which someone usually will, then you can rephrase the question to see if that helps get people talking.

- **Resist the urge to offer answers or advice.** Just because you are the group leader does not mean it is up to you to answer questions posed in the group. Let questions be opportunities for deeper discussion. The same goes for advice. Often a group dynamic can turn into offering one member advice based on something that person said. Steer participants away from advice-giving unless someone has explicitly asked for it. If someone shares something difficult with the group, the person likely just wants to be heard, not preached to.

- **Give quieter participants room to talk.** Most groups have members who are comfortable sharing and members who are more hesitant to share. Do not rely on the most communicative members of the group to carry your discussion. Give everyone an opportunity to share. You can do this by choosing one question in which you go around the circle so everyone can share. Or if you have noticed one side of the room or circle is quieter than the other, you could say, "Let us hear from this side of the room." Do not call on individuals directly, as this can feel intimidating for someone who is hesitant to share. Instead, gently invite everyone to participate.
- **Pray.** One of the most powerful tools you have as a group leader is prayer. Pray before your group time, pray for the other participants throughout the week, and pray that you will be attuned to the Spirit and where He wants the conversation to go. When your group is covered in prayer, it's amazing to watch what God can do.

The Go and Do Section

Each session concludes with a Go and Do section. Please do not skip this part of your group time! Since the purpose of this study is to equip and empower people of faith to engage with those who are experiencing homelessness, this section is how you can hold each other accountable to action, rather than just words.

Your group action item does not have to be grandiose or complicated. Here are a few ideas:

- Have participants call local organizations who work with homelessness and ask what resources they are lacking. Maybe your group could help fill that need.
- Commit to praying for one person you know who is experiencing homelessness. See if the Spirit prompts you to help that person in some way.

- Choose a Saturday morning that your group could volunteer together at your local Salvation Army, rescue mission, or another organization you know is engaging homelessness in a meaningful way.
- Research local political candidates and how they plan to tackle the issue of homelessness. At your next group time, discuss what you learned. Be sensitive to varying political opinions in the group. Keep the conversation based on the issue of homelessness rather than political party.

Jesus said, "Where two or three gather in my name, there am I with them" (Matthew 18:20). Trust that Jesus will be with you during each session. He has a plan for your group. Everyone who is there is there for a reason. Your job is simply to create a welcoming environment for your group to meet, for the teachings of Jesus to be shared, and for the Holy Spirit to move.

Access the Videos Here
Link: https://DavidCCook.org/access
Access Code: ADDRESS
Or scan this QR code:

Session 1

Come as You Are

Dr. Robert G. Marbut Jr.

Former White House "Federal Homelessness Czar," Founding President/
CEO of Haven for Hope, and Discovery Institute Senior Fellow

Rev. Brandan Thomas

Former CEO at Winchester Rescue Mission and Director of Leadership,
Learning, and Program for Citygate Network

The Gospels are filled with examples of Jesus meeting people where they are. Accepting us as we are, while loving us too much to leave us as we are.

Jesus interacts with those who have stumbled, the broken and hurting. Jesus came to create a way for us to reconnect with the Father *and* to show us a better way to live.

Jesus Meets Us Where We Are

In the gospel of John, Jesus was traveling to Jerusalem for a feast when He came to the pool of Bethesda. Surrounded by five covered colonnades, the pool was always crowded with people who were blind, lame, paralyzed, or otherwise disabled. Tradition held that, from time to time, an angel would come and stir the waters. If you were the first in the pool after the water was stirred, you would be healed.

In this story, Jesus saw a man who had been disabled for thirty-eight years lying near the pool. When Jesus asked him if he wanted to be healed, the man responded, "I have no one to help me into the pool when the water is stirred. While I am trying to get in, someone else goes down ahead of me."

This man had bought into the idea that making it into the pool would bring healing. He believed it would happen only if someone could help him. His frustration was not that it had yet to happen, but *that no one would help make it happen.*

Jesus told him to get up, pick up his mat, and walk. The man did what Jesus instructed and was healed immediately. After years of being focused on the pool, he no longer was interested in the pool itself, because Jesus had provided the thing the pool never produced for him: healing. Jesus made it happen.

> ## Jesus had provided the thing the pool never produced for him: healing. *Jesus made it happen.*

This story shows both the power Jesus has to meet the hurting right where they are and His uncompromising love and commitment to not leave the hurting where they are.

The man who had been disabled for thirty-eight years had no hope of being healed. In fact, he had been stuck because he had placed all his hope in a healing that was not possible. Yet, he was healed once he encountered Jesus. Likewise, no matter how long we have been suffering, Jesus meets His people where we are and as we are, but He does not stop there. He loves us too much to leave us as He found us.

Meeting Others Where They Are

Often people experiencing homelessness are in a chronic state of homelessness, and not simply because they have lost a job or fallen into tough times. Many have undiagnosed and therefore untreated mental illnesses along with self-medicating substance use issues. And while lack of housing is a major factor in homelessness, we must look at the full picture.

The California Policy Lab, a nonpartisan research institute based at the University of California, found that 78 percent of the people experiencing unsheltered homelessness (i.e., "street-level" homelessness) reported having mental health conditions, and 50 percent said their mental health conditions had contributed to their loss of housing. Additionally, 75 percent of the unsheltered population reported having substance abuse conditions, and 51 percent said the use of drugs or alcohol had contributed to their loss of housing.[1]

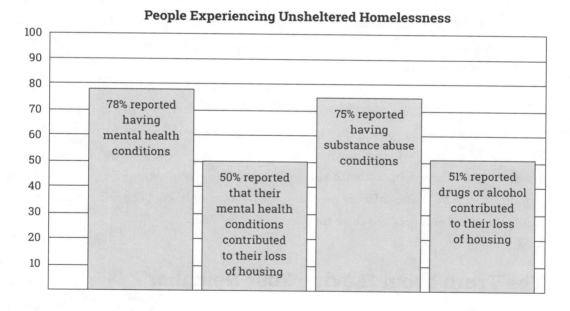

Individuals experiencing homelessness and untreated mental illness attempt to numb their pain by self-medicating with alcohol, opioids, meth, fentanyl, and other legal and illegal drugs. Many people who come to centers like the Winchester Rescue Mission in Winchester, Virginia, and Haven for Hope in San Antonio, Texas, say that alcohol and drugs "help" their mental illness. Their belief is they can self-medicate their way to healing, or at least temporarily forget the issues of the day. Sadly, this keeps these individuals enslaved to addiction, isolation, and homelessness.

Jerome[2] came to Winchester Rescue Mission after a judge remanded him to custody. Diagnosed with paranoid schizophrenia in 2007, Jerome did well when he took his prescription medications. But he often failed to take them, choosing to self-medicate by other means. Jerome bounced between homelessness and serving jail time for crimes he committed when he was not taking his prescribed medications.

At the Mission, Jerome found not only a welcoming and loving environment but also invaluable support from case managers, clinical counselors, and medication management professionals. This support helped prevent him from returning to his unhealthy habits. After meeting his basic needs, he was encouraged to learn more about the God who empowers us and how to exit homelessness. Jerome determined that he would listen, learn, and take his meds. As a result, he stabilized and then began to thrive. Today, Jerome mentors other men experiencing homelessness and says, "I'm no longer defined by my disease."

When followers of Christ take Jesus's approach to simply meet people where they are, it is a game changer. We must also love individuals and support their change and improvement, not enabling them to stay the way they arrived. When Jesus approached the man at the pool of Bethesda, He did not try to convince him that the pool theory would not work. Instead, Jesus first got to know the man by talking to him, looking him in the eyes, asking him questions, then providing him with exactly what he needed in the moment so he could envision living a new life—a life he had only dreamed about for thirty-eight long years.

The Truth about "Loving Your Neighbor"

Sometimes we help someone by meeting their simplest of needs and sending them on their way. But other times it takes a bigger investment of resources and time, much like the story of the Good Samaritan in Luke 10.

The story begins with a lawyer asking Jesus what he had to do to inherit eternal life. Jesus responded by asking the lawyer what was written in the Law. "Love the Lord your God with all your heart and with all your soul and with all your strength and with all your mind; and, 'Love your neighbor as yourself,'" the lawyer said.

After Jesus agreed that the lawyer had answered correctly, the man asked, "Who is my neighbor?" Jesus responded with a story that involves the investment of resources, time, energy, risk taking, and of course, love.

A man traveling from Jerusalem to Jericho was attacked by robbers who beat him, took his clothes, and left him half dead. A priest and then a Levite each passed by, but neither stopped to help him—in fact, after assessing the situation, they both took extra effort to avoid the injured traveler by crossing to the other side of the road. Finally, a Samaritan came along and, seeing the man, took mercy on him, bandaged his wounds, and carried him to an inn to receive additional care. "Look after him," he told the innkeeper, "and when I return, I will reimburse you for any extra expenses."

This story teaches us the importance of "loving your neighbor" regardless of who that person is. Jesus takes exceptional care to leave out any identifying attributes of the man who was beaten. It is impossible to assume anything about the victim's social status, nationality, lifestyle, or religious affiliation. Omitting these clues prevents us from making assumptions about why the man was on the road and what help he truly needed.

The priest and Levite seemed to make hasty judgments without taking the time to fully understand the situation. As religious leaders, they may have felt obligated to adhere to societal expectations or rules around ritual purity that discouraged interactions with those considered unclean or impure—such as a wounded person. Ironically, these social norms, although misguided, may have played a role in shaping their response to the man in need.

Additionally, the priest and Levite may have held biased views about individuals traveling that road or those of different social or ethnic backgrounds, especially in the land of Samaria, which may have also contributed to their unwillingness to help. Biases can develop based on stereotypes or generalizations about certain groups of people, leading to a tendency to make snap judgments without considering the individual circumstances.

Rather than succumbing to hasty judgments, the Samaritan assessed the situation, set aside any biases, and prioritized the immediate needs of the wounded man. The Samaritan—the outcast—was the one who showed compassion and met the beaten man's needs right where he was. He bandaged the traveler's wounds, put him on his own donkey, and took him to an inn to be cared for. Maybe that was enough, right?

The Samaritan loved the wounded traveler as he was, but he loved him too much to allow him to go unattended on the side of the road in the short term and untreated at the inn over the long term.

Yet the Samaritan challenged himself to go even deeper ... to invest in a stranger, a neighbor, telling the innkeeper, "Take care of this man.... If his bill runs higher than this, I will pay you the next time I am here." The Samaritan knew it was not enough to leave the man where he was.

The hasty judgments made by the priest and Levite serve as a reminder of the dangers of making assumptions without gathering adequate information or considering the broader context. Their actions highlight the importance of examining our own biases, challenging societal norms, and cultivating a mindset of true empathy and compassion.

As James wrote:

> My brothers and sisters, believers in our glorious Lord Jesus Christ must not show favoritism. Suppose a man comes into your meeting wearing a gold ring and fine clothes, and a poor man in filthy old clothes also comes in. If you show special attention to the man wearing fine clothes and say, "Here's a good seat for you," but say to the poor man, "You stand there" or "Sit on the floor by my feet," have you not discriminated among yourselves and become judges with evil thoughts? (2:1–4)

This passage reminds us of the importance of seeing beyond stereotypes and prejudice. It challenges us to recognize the inherent worth and humanity of every individual, regardless of their situation. By embracing compassion, we can overcome biases and treat all people with the dignity and respect they deserve.

Meaningful Engagement

For many Christians, offering meals and a warm bed (what individuals experiencing homelessness often refer to as "three hots and a cot") is the start *and* end of their compassion story. Food and sleep are important, but it is not the whole story. Maslow's Hierarchy of Needs identifies food and shelter as basic needs but reminds us of more essential human needs such as safety and self-esteem.[3] Long before Abraham Maslow formulated his theory, Jesus recognized that meeting physiological needs was just the beginning. We also need connection, accomplishment, purpose, meaning, and love.

We also need connection, accomplishment, purpose, meaning, and love.

The parable of the Good Samaritan provides a powerful lesson on the importance of extending compassion and offering long-term support to those experiencing homelessness. By taking the beaten man to an inn and collaborating with the innkeeper to care for the man in need, the Good Samaritan exemplified the significance of sustained assistance, financial provision, and building relationships.

In today's world, this story encourages us to go beyond immediate aid of three hots and a cot and engage in efforts that address the root causes of suffering and homelessness by providing ongoing support and empowerment. "Meaningful engagement"—a concept you will see throughout this study—is the best way the church can help in the face of what often feels like a hopeless situation.

We often make snap judgments about people experiencing homelessness. We stereotype these individuals as lazy or lacking ambition. We think "they" *chose* homelessness; they could improve their situation if they would just try harder; or they are responsible for their situation. But in developed countries like the US, homelessness results from a combination of factors such as self-medicating mental health issues, poor medical care, and inadequate education.

To meaningfully engage homelessness, we must understand its root causes, address each person as an individual with a unique journey that led to where they are today, and then collaborate to provide the long-term help they need.

This is what the Good Samaritan did. His love transcended societal barriers, showing compassion and acceptance for a stranger in need. He saw the immediate need for medical attention and took immediate action, and he also saw the long-term needs for safe shelter and continued medical help.

Could This Be Your Church?

In a small town, nestled amidst rolling hills, a humble church called Grace Community Church formed. The congregation had a grassroots calling to love and serve people experiencing homelessness in their community. They understood that their mission was not just to provide the temporary relief of food and a mattress, but to offer a transformative and holistic approach to those experiencing homelessness, even those struggling with addiction and mental illness.

Loving the families and individuals suffering the effects of homelessness meant creating a welcoming environment of dignity and respect, with the complexities and challenges of each person. **The church leadership began by educating their members about the importance of using *people-first* language—emphasizing the individual's worth beyond their circumstances.** They encouraged seeing *the person* before he or she was inflicted by addiction or mental health issues, recognizing each person as traveling a unique journey with unknowns around every corner, and acknowledging the truth of "there but for the grace of God go I."

John walked through the doors of Grace Community Church's safe and welcoming ministry after being directed there by another service agency. He had been battling substance abuse for several agonizing years. His life journey began full of hope. He had a job that covered his rent, utilities, a car payment, and other bills. He had family and friends. But as he looked for a little more excitement—a little more happiness—he started partying. After a few years, drug and alcohol addiction took him by surprise and John lost everything due to his life choices.

When he got to the church ministry via a referral of a sister service agency, John was greeted with open arms and genuine care. Just as the Good Samaritan met the immediate needs of the man beaten on the road, Grace Community Church volunteers jumped in to treat John's most visible needs for food, rest, a shower, and fresh clothing.

As John's broken body responded to the compassionate care he received, he became open to the possibility of change. Grace Community Church's team provided him with information about a local rehabilitation program and connected him with a support group that helped him navigate the challenges of recovery. But they did not stop there.

John began a new journey, this time to sobriety, and the church continued to offer him unwavering support. They provided him with a safe and stable living environment, connecting him with mentors who walked alongside him and helped him develop new skills for employment. They celebrated his milestones, offering encouragement during challenges and empowering him to build a future free from addiction.

Grace Community Church approached its service to those experiencing homelessness by creating a holistic program that met people where they were and provided them with the means to overcome life-dominating barriers to success. They *meaningfully engaged* with those who were experiencing homelessness. They did this by:

- Starting with providing essential services such as food, showers, fresh clothing, and rest.
- Then addressing the underlying causes of homelessness by partnering with local treatment centers for substance use disorder and mental health challenges.
- Organizing counseling sessions, support groups, and workshops on addiction recovery.
- Offering case management, job training, and life-skills development.

The church also recognized that everyone, sheltered or unsheltered, needs community and connection, a need to simply belong. John attended regular gatherings with participants from the church and from the homelessness community, sharing meals, stories, and laughter. These opportunities to fellowship erased the lines between the sheltered and the unsheltered, and drew everyone together in the common goal of learning, healing, and growing.

The Good Samaritan was committed to the beaten man's long-term needs no matter the cost. In the same way, the church ministry members recognized the cost of showing Jesus-centric compassion to the hurting individuals who entered their doors. They refused to enable destructive behaviors, choosing instead to provide empathetic support while maintaining healthy boundaries, a *smart-love* approach. They recognized that true love requires collaboratively guiding individuals toward professional help and resources rather than perpetuating a cycle of dependence. Smart love works.

The Good News

This true story serves as a model for churches and communities seeking to love families and individuals experiencing homelessness where they are without enabling the behaviors that led to their homelessness. By offering dignity and respect, creating a supportive environment, providing resources for recovery and rehabilitation, and maintaining healthy boundaries, they demonstrated that true love involves both compassion and accountability.

Through their holistic approach, Grace Community Church not only helped individuals experiencing homelessness find stability and healing, but they also cultivated a community that understood the power of love and its transformative impact. They embodied the message that God loves us as we are but loves us too much to let us stay as we are.

Homelessness is a major challenge, but it is one that we can address. There are about 600,000 people experiencing "street-level" homelessness in the United States, and there are about 350,000 congregations in the United States. What would happen if every church in the United States worked with just one or two people experiencing homelessness? Think about the impact your congregation could have.

Adult Homelessness 101

John Ashmen

Past President of Citygate Network

Adapted from his book Invisible Neighbors

Homelessness has skyrocketed in the United States over the last decade and has reached crisis levels in many American cities. This is a human tragedy for the individuals and their families caught up in the heartbreaking cycle of despair.

Exactly how many of our neighbors across the United States are experiencing homelessness is hard to determine. The numbers can be confusing and misleading, primarily because governmental definitions and rules for counting those suffering keep changing, sometimes to shield politicians from the realities on the streets or to promote favored policies.

Counting and understanding homelessness can be complicated. In order to successfully address the challenges of homelessness, we must first have an accurate understanding of the issue.

What Is Homelessness?

The federal government has two definitions of *homelessness*, as well as two different sets of methodologies and metrics to measure the number of people experiencing homelessness. The US Department of Housing and Urban Development (HUD) primarily tracks adults, while the US Department of Education (ED) tracks child and youth homelessness.

HUD's general definition of a person experiencing homelessness is one who "lacks a fixed, regular, and adequate nighttime residence."[4] HUD groups individuals experiencing homelessness into five sub-categories or cohorts, based on current housing type:

1. Unsheltered (also known as street-level homelessness or "sleeping rough")
2. Emergency Shelters (like Citygate Network missions and Salvation Army centers)
3. Transitional Housing (subsidized apartments with wraparound services for up to two years)
4. Rapid Rehousing (subsidized housing with no program participation requirements)
5. Permanent Supportive Housing (longer-term subsidized housing units with no program participation requirements)

How We Talk about Homelessness Matters

Compiling all five cohorts of homelessness, there are almost 1.2 million individuals experiencing homelessness per the HUD definition. Cohorts 1 and 2—unsheltered and in emergency shelters—are often grouped together and called un-housed or "street-level" homeless. This group is about 600,000 individuals, as reported by the media. Most frontline service-providing agencies feel these numbers grossly undercount the actual number of adults experiencing homelessness.

A good case can be made that there are more than 2 million *adults* experiencing all types of homelessness in the United States on any given night (this does not include families with children which is addressed elsewhere). To put it into perspective: that's the number of people it would take to fill *every* seat in *every* NFL stadium in the United States at the *same time*.

Regardless of the debate over definition and counting, most agree that overall homelessness is increasing across the United States, and a growing number of communities are in a crisis. Many mayors, particularly in West Coast cities, have declared public disaster emergencies because of the magnitude of the overall suffering on the streets.

Affordable Housing Is Only Part of the Story

The lack of affordable housing is commonly cited as the main cause of homelessness. Housing costs and available inventory certainly have a major bearing on the situation, but there's more to the story. For a better understanding, consider this background information.

Starting in 2013, programmatic changes required by the HUD NOFA (Notice of Funding Availability) penalized service agencies and programs that included service participation requirements. HUD funding guidelines prioritized speed of placement (e.g., how fast a person received a key to a subsidized housing unit) rather than quality of placement (e.g., can the person successfully maintain sustainable housing). This resulted in replacing high-quality recovery and rehabilitative programs—often faith-based—with subsidized housing programs that were absent of participation requirements for treatment programs. In essence, it created a federal homelessness assistance program that is functionally equivalent to Section 8 housing (federally subsidized housing) with no rules, no treatment programs, and no participation requirements. The "Housing First" initiative was born.

It is important to note that prior to the implementation of Housing First, the total number of *unsheltered* individuals had dropped 31.4 percent between 2007 and 2014, when intensive wraparound services for participants were required for most homelessness assistance program participants. The downward trend ended with HUD's adoption of the Housing First approach.[5]

Mental Illness Is a Big Factor

In the 1960s and 1970s, there was a movement to do away with "insane asylums." Many of these mental health facilities had become overcrowded with horrible conditions that led to abuse of the patients. During this time, many elected officials also thought the federal government should not be funding mental health services, so most of the asylums in the United States were defunded and closed. Since then, the number of in-patient treatment beds for people with mental illness has dropped by more than 90 percent.

Community-based treatment was touted to be the modern solution for serving those with mental illness. While ending the asylum mayhem was a decent thing to do, this replacement plan was never properly funded and did not work. Instead, many individuals with untreated mental illness are now living on the streets, showing up in emergency rooms, and filling jails.

Substance Abuse Disorders and Addiction Are Prevalent

Untreated mental illness often leads to self-medication, especially by people who live on the street and are trying to numb the effects of extreme weather conditions, high levels of noise, physical abuse, insects, and rats, just to name a few of the horrific issues that come with homelessness.

All of the drugs you have heard about (and some you have not) are available on the streets, for the right price or the right favor. Fentanyl has become the newest drug of choice and is fifty times more powerful than heroin and one hundred times more powerful than morphine.[6] Because of its drop in street price and new "cocktail mixtures," fentanyl is now the deadliest drug ever to reach the streets.

> "For I was hungry and you gave me something to eat, I was thirsty and you gave me something to drink, I was a stranger and you invited me in, I needed clothes and you clothed me, I was sick and you looked after me, I was in prison and you came to visit me."
> Matthew 25:35–36

Alcohol continues to be commonly abused, primarily because of its accessibility. Studies show that alcoholics who are experiencing homelessness typically began drinking in their youth. One report, published in the Annals of Emergency Medicine, details research conducted at Bellevue Hospital in New York City. It showed that "one hundred percent of patients enrolled in the study began drinking alcohol as children, becoming alcohol-dependent shortly thereafter." Study author Dr. Ryan McCormack noted, "For people who have homes and jobs, it is difficult to imagine the level of despair these people experience day in and day out, or the all-consuming focus on getting the next drink that overrides even the most basic human survival instinct."[7]

The gospel of Matthew could not be clearer that anyone who desires to follow Jesus has a responsibly to help the poor and oppressed (Matthew 25:31–40). Also explicit in the New Testament is that the "church" is a divinely chosen channel to nurture and empower saints to do kingdom work (Ephesians 4:11–13). In short, the church has an enormous and enduring social obligation. Sadly, in many respects, the church has surrendered much of its charge to the government.

Wait, There's More

Untreated mental illness, addiction, and lack of affordable housing are the big logs that keep the homelessness fire raging. But there's more fueling this national problem. There's family dysfunction, lack of education, joblessness, PTSD, human trafficking, young people aging out of the foster care system, LGBTQ kids running away from home or being thrown out—the list goes on and on. Clearly, homelessness is a multifaceted problem that needs a multifaceted solution.

While government, despite red-tape entanglement and a bit of misguided compassion, tries its best to end people's physical poverty, it can't end their spiritual and relational poverty. It's not in the government's purview. That is where the church must step in.

The Church Has a Changing History with Homelessness

From the frontier days through the US Civil War, individual churches, large or small, were the driving force in homelessness ministry. They cared for the widows and orphans in their communities and opened soup kitchens to feed those who were not getting enough to eat.

The global conflict of World War II changed everything. Hundreds of thousands of people, mostly men, who had never ventured more than a few miles away from their homes, found themselves on the other side of the world, involved in the carnage of war. Many had epiphanies and "foxhole conversions" that reshaped their lives: "God, get me out of here in one piece and I will follow and serve You and commit my life to correcting these terrible wrongs." Many lived up to their prayers.

The decade following World War II saw the start of thousands of ministries independent of existing churches. Many of them went on to be evangelical household names: Billy Graham Evangelistic Association, World Vision, Young Life, Youth for Christ, and hundreds more.

As a result, a new paradigm emerged. Socially active ministry was no longer local-church or denominationally driven. Although single churches and denominations still had their unique influence, it was now by and large "parachurch" driven, by ministries coming alongside the church.

In many cases "professionals" were now in charge of hands-on ministries. Anyone could join the ranks, but serious involvement customarily required a change of vocation. Unfortunately, many average church attendees felt pushed away from the front line of action and service. And that took a toll on local church engagement. This remained the case for the next several decades.

Recently, the paradigm started shifting again, and the front lines are now clearly in sight to individual Christ followers who are not waiting for congregational sanctioning. These ministries are cause-driven, youth-led, and technology-enhanced. They are focused on issues like clean water, global hunger, human trafficking, literacy, and the like, with the gospel as the catalyst. More and more are now looking at the serious issues in our downtowns and neighborhoods.

Could this be the dawn of a new day of engagement for the church—particularly in the areas of compassionate ministries to individuals and families experiencing homelessness? Many believe so, especially because of the involvement of so many younger people who see their faith as more communal than personal. The questions are: Can this be sustained? And will you be part of this movement?

Child and Family Homelessness 101

Barbara Duffield

Executive Director of SchoolHouse Connection

When you hear the word *homeless* or *homelessness*, the image that may first come to mind is of a single adult man on the street of a large city. However, the reality is that millions of children and youth also experience homelessness with their families each year. According to the US Department of Education (ED), pre-COVID, there were almost 1.5 million children experiencing homelessness.[8] This number did not include infants and toddlers who were too young for school, or children and youth who were not enrolled in school or had dropped out. The prevalence of youth homelessness is comparable in rural, suburban, and urban areas.[9]

The relationships between parents, and between parents and children, are important dynamics that make family homelessness unique and different from that of single-adult homelessness. Parents have their unique needs as individuals, but also as caretakers: physical space, material resources, and emotional capacities of parenting. Children and youth of every age, from infancy through adolescence, also have unique developmental needs: physical, social, emotional, and spiritual.

Programs and policies designed to address family homelessness must provide holistic, integrated support to break the generational cycle of homelessness. It is very important to note that many homeless adults first experienced homelessness as children or youth, then failed to graduate from high school, and/or suffered various adverse events that impacted them throughout life.[10]

Efforts to intervene before these children and youth reached adulthood could have prevented their later bouts of more entrenched homelessness.

Family Homelessness Causes	**Youth Homelessness Causes**
domestic violence	history of family homelessness
low education levels	physical and sexual abuse
financial loss tied to divorce and family separation	neglect
shortage of affordable housing	parental substance abuse
unemployment	physical and mental health problems
deep poverty	addiction disorders
	natural disasters
	extreme family conflict[11]

"I was 8 years old when I first experienced homelessness.... I still have flashbacks to the many months my family lived in motels, and how my classmates had the basic necessities that I did not have. Constantly moving and being disappointed led me to become extremely detached and avoid relationships of any kind out of fear of abandonment. Eight years later, at 16 years old, I was still experiencing homelessness."

Jahnee S., a child who has experienced homelessness

Family homelessness is a complex and traumatic experience with long-term consequences, particularly for children and youth in their most critical stages of development. Yet homelessness among families with children is often hidden, and is a very different type of homelessness compared to single adults. Relative to single adults experiencing homelessness, families with children are significantly more likely to be negatively affected by the cost of housing. Lack of shelter and fear of having children removed from parental custody mean that most families experiencing homelessness stay in places that are not easily identified.

Of the children and youth identified as experiencing homelessness and enrolled in public schools in the 2021–2022 school year, only 11 percent were staying in shelters when they were first identified as homeless, 9 percent were staying in motels, and 4 percent were staying in unsheltered locations. The rest (76 percent) were staying with other people temporarily due to loss of housing, economic hardship, or a similar reason.[12] These situations—which are included in the ED's legal definition of *homelessness*—are precarious, damaging, crowded, unstable, and often unsafe, leading to extraordinary rates of mobility.

Responding to Family Homelessness

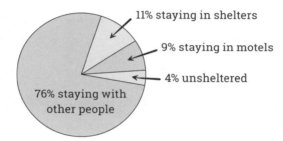

Families experiencing homelessness are a distinct population with specific needs that require a different approach than single-adult homelessness.

In considering how to help families and children in your community, start by learning what resources and programs already exist. While existing resources vary tremendously, one universal source of support for families experiencing homelessness may surprise you: public schools. Federal law requires public schools and federally funded early childhood programs to identify children and youth experiencing homelessness and remove barriers to their enrollment and success.[13] These are the only federal programs that have the responsibility for and expertise in finding, engaging, and serving these students and upholding their educational rights.

Under the McKinney-Vento Act, every school district must designate a liaison to identify homeless children and youth, ensure school access and stability, provide direct services, and coordinate with community agencies to meet basic needs. Contacting your school district's homelessness liaison is one way to learn about the most pressing current needs, as well as about community-based school partners.

"[The counselor from my service agency] helped me get my driver's license, helped me pay for gas to get to school, gave me money for food, and even had someone come and talk to me and just ask me if I was okay on a weekly basis. A local service agency showed interest in me, they believed in my potential, they cared about me. It felt like there was an army of angels standing beside me from that day forward. I'll never forget the simple act of one of my teachers opening their classroom to me an hour before school started just so I could have breakfast with them and talk. To the agency and my teacher these were small acts of kindness, but to me they were so significant. They helped me find the courage to get help."

Rebecca C., a child who has experienced homelessness

Keep in mind:

- Families who experience homelessness may attend your church but don't know that help is available or are ashamed to let anyone know their situation. It is important to publicize resources so families can seek help in a safe, dignified way.

- Parents who experience homelessness often struggle with depression, feeling they have failed as parents to provide for their children. It is important to affirm their role as parents and provide support for the entire family.

- Lack of safe, affordable childcare and transportation can be tremendous barriers for parents who are seeking employment, treatment, or housing. Identify gaps in local childcare and transportation services, and find out how you can volunteer to help fill them.

- Children and youth who experience homelessness need stability and crave normalcy. Items and activities that allow them to participate fully in school and extracurricular activities help deepen their connections to peers, allow them to explore who they are outside of their homelessness, and offer respite from the upheaval in their lives.

- Adolescents who are part of families experiencing homelessness often become caretakers for their younger siblings, and even their parents. This adds even more stress and pressure to the usual challenges of adolescence. Consider specific outreach and support for teens, who might otherwise be overlooked.

- The health and developmental needs of infants and toddlers also must be addressed specifically and intentionally, from nutrition, to safe and adequate spaces to crawl and explore, to activities that promote healthy attachment.

- Children, youth, and families who experience homelessness contend with grief, loss, and isolation. It's important to adopt a trauma-informed approach to supportive activities and offer counseling, mentorship, and services that promote healing.

In sum, families with children who experience homelessness are less visible than homeless single adults, but are more vulnerable. Strategies must account for their unique needs and be prioritized as both a crisis response and a prevention strategy in order to reduce the cycle of homelessness among all Americans.

Session 1 Group Guide
Welcome

Welcome to session 1's group guide of the *No Address Interactive Study Guide*. If you and your group members don't already know one another, take some time to introduce yourselves. You can watch the Overview video (see next page) now or after you answer the following questions:

1. What experience do you have with homelessness in your community?

2. What do you hope to learn from this study?

Watch

Hopefully you had a chance to read about how Jesus meets us where we are and how we can meet those who are experiencing homelessness where they are with compassion and love rather than judgment.

> **Watch the Session 1 Overview and Intro videos.**
> **(Note: This session's videos will be longer than the rest. You can access the videos via the QR code or link on page 36.)**

Discussion

Discuss what you watched from the video and the material you read this week using the following questions as a guide.

1. How have you felt welcomed by a "come as you are" philosophy within your church or community? What has it felt like to *not* feel welcomed?

2. How can the church meet people where they are, while encouraging them not to stay that way? What have you seen done well in your church or community? What could be done better?

3. When you picture someone who is experiencing homelessness, who do you see? Where does this image come from?

4. How has your understanding of the connections—and differences—between adult and child homelessness changed?

5. Did any of the statistics or facts about the millions of adults and children who are experiencing homelessness make you feel overwhelmed? If so, which ones, and why?

What Does the Bible Say?

1. Read John 5:1–8. How did Jesus meet the lame man where he was? How has Jesus met you during a difficult time in your life?

2. How have you judged people who are experiencing homelessness? How could meeting them where they are foster compassion rather than judgment?

3. Read Luke 10:25–37. Has anyone ever offered you long-term love and compassion in this way? If so, who? And how did this person's love affect you?

4. Read 2 Corinthians 12:9–10. What does Christ do with our weakness? What does this mean for us when we feel paralyzed by major issues like homelessness?

5. Many children are born into a cycle of homelessness, impacting generations. Read Proverbs 22:6. How has the way you were raised affected you? How does this help you understand the generational cycle of homelessness?

6. Read Psalm 139:13–17. How does God feel about us, even before we're born? What does this tell you about how God feels about children who are experiencing homelessness and, in turn, how we should view them?

Go and Do

> **Watch the Session 1 Wrap-up video.**
> **(You can access the video via the QR code or link on page 36.)**

What can you do as a group and individually this week to apply what you learned about homelessness?

This week, **we** will:

This week, **I** will:

Pray

End your time by sharing prayer requests and praying for one another to feel equipped and encouraged to engage those who are experiencing homelessness. Record prayer requests below or in the journal pages at the end of the book, so you can continue to pray for one another throughout the week.

For Next Week

Read Session 2 on pages 63–73.

If you want to learn more about this week's topics, check out the following resources:

- John Ashmen, "Concerning Statistics," chapter 2 in *Invisible Neighbors* (San Clemente, CA: CrossSection, 2017).
- *Americans with No Address* documentary
- SchoolHouse Connection, "The Issue," https://schoolhouseconnection.org /the-issue/.

- Barbara Duffield, "Reimagining Homelessness Assistance for Children and Families," *Journal of Children and Poverty*, September 1, 2020, DOI: 10.1080/10796126.2020.1813535.
- Discovery Institute, "How Congress Can Reform Government's Misguided Homelessness Policies," www.discovery.org/m/securepdfs/2022/10/How-Congress-Can-Reform-Governments-Misguided-Homelessness-Policies-20221011.pdf.
- National Center for Homeless Education, US Department of Education, "Annual Federal Data Summary School Years—Education for Homeless Children and Youth," https://nche.ed.gov/data-and-stats/.

Reflect

Use the questions below to reflect on your "go and do" action item this week.

1. Describe your "go and do" task for the week. What did you do? Who did you meet?

2. What did you learn about the state of homelessness in your community?

3. What did you learn about Jesus?

4. What did you learn about yourself?

Session 2

Engage, Don't Enable

Dr. Roxanne Jordan

Senior Vice President of Programs for Los Angeles Mission and Anne Douglas Center for Women

Engaging Homelessness

In Mark 14:7, Jesus said, "The poor you will always have with you, and you can help them any time you want. But you will not always have me." He said this immediately following the loving act of a woman who chose to spare no expense in anointing Him with a costly oil before His forthcoming burial. While the disciples who witnessed this act grumbled that she should not have wasted such a precious gift on Him, to Jesus it was clear the woman had her priorities in order: Jesus first, then the needs of others.

This is what Jesus commanded in Mark 12: "'Love the Lord your God with all your heart and with all your soul and with all your mind and with all your strength.' The second [most important commandment] is this: 'Love your neighbor as yourself'" (verses 30–31).

Jesus knew that He would not always be with the disciples in bodily form. He would be crucified, buried, and resurrected, thus sending the Holy Spirit to His disciples to manifest His kingdom on earth. The question for them and for us is how do we allow Jesus's commandment of love to manifest in our day-to-day lives among the poor, the needy, or those experiencing homelessness in our society, not in a legalistic way, but in the power of the Holy Spirit?

I believe the best way to love our neighbors who are experiencing homelessness as Jesus commanded is through *engaging* rather than *enabling* homelessness.

Engage vs. Enable

The Oxford Dictionary defines *engage* as a verb meaning "to occupy, attract, or involve someone's interest or attention, or to participate or become involved in." Merriam-Webster defines the term this way: "to offer something, such as one's life or a word as backing up a cause or aim, to attract and hold by influence or power, to be committed to or supportive of a cause."

In comparison, *enable* is defined as "supporting adverse or dysfunctional behavior."[1]

In the context of addiction, which as you know by now is one of the primary causes of street-level homelessness, enabling means doing something for someone they can and should be doing for themselves, which often makes the situation worse.

When friends and family enable their loved ones, they function as a cushion, preventing the addicted person from facing the consequences of their substance abuse. Many times a loved one enables an addiction (often unknowingly), causing the addicted person to lose faith in themselves and not respect the loved ones who make it easier for them to continue using drugs.

With the high rates of addiction in this country, most family members and professionals in the field are fully aware of *the high cost of enabling behaviors*:

denial

lack of accountability

justification

suppressed feelings

avoidance of the problem

protecting the family image

playing the blame game

controlling behaviors

minimizing the situation

or assuming responsibilities, to name a few

On the other hand, *strategic and intentional engagement promotes*:

recovery

self-sufficiency

accountability

healthy structures

developmental and interpersonal change

rehabilitation

spiritual formation

vocational development

relational wellness

the possibility for social, economic,

and political reform

You may not realize when you're enabling homelessness. Consider the examples below.

Enabling ⟹	Engaging
"Street-feeding"—handing out food in a park, within an encampment, or on the street—perpetuates the challenges of homelessness by discouraging and distracting people from joining a treatment program. Additionally, the lack of training in safely handling food can cause cases of food poisoning. Finally, the food delivered via street-feeding is often non-nutritious, which is neither respectful nor dignifying.	Instead of street-feeding, help prepare and deliver meals within a clean facility at an existing, successful program that has holistic wraparound services. These programs typically provide nineteen to twenty-one meals per week that are part of an overall nutritiously balanced meal plan with significantly higher standards of food-safety handling and delivery. Volunteering within a high-quality treatment center improves nutrition, reduces food poisoning, and encourages people experiencing homelessness to enter into treatment.
Enabling ⟹	**Engaging**
Handing out cash to a person on the street is actually one of the worst actions a person can take since, more often than not, the cash funds negative habits such as purchasing drugs and alcohol, or prostitution. No one would consider handing out fentanyl to an addict or a six-pack of beer to an alcoholic, yet this is exactly what occurs with cash given out on the street. Every time this has been studied, more than 90 percent of the cash given out goes directly to drugs, alcohol, and prostitution.	Rather than giving cash to a person on the street, make a tax-deductible donation to a high-quality homelessness service agency such as The Salvation Army or a Citygate Rescue Mission. Faith-based and non-profit programs depend on gifts to sustain operations. Instead of giving out $3 every week, make a $150 donation to a well-run program.

These examples of engagement embody the definition we discussed above. They allow you to show interest and attention, participate, become involved, and use your power, meaning your resources, talent, and time.

Holistic Services That Engage Rather Than Enable

It is a privilege to work daily with individuals, parents, and families who enter our twelve-month Fresh Start Rehabilitation program at the Anne Douglas Center for Women within the Los Angeles Mission (LAM). There they receive hot meals, clean clothes, and personal hygiene items, and are able to shower with dignity. They often come to the center to be *engaged*—greeted by the staff, welcomed with a smile, a kind gesture, a prayer, or a mere word of encouragement that fosters self-esteem and hope.

In our program, I have seen a thirty-year-old woman who was molested from the age of six, who had four children in the "system," and had been addicted to heroin for fifteen years, enter our doors, learn about God's love for her, receive salvation, experience sobriety, become stable enough to obtain housing, and regain a relationship with her children. I have witnessed firsthand God's engagement with people through programs, organizations, and systems.

At the LAM, our mission is to "break the cycle of homelessness and poverty by stabilizing people in a safe and spiritual environment, connecting them to solutions and walking with them on their journey." We are committed to helping solve the underlying essential and pressing social issues of homelessness and poverty through an innovative and sustainable model. We created a complete program of safe and spiritual shelter, dignified self-empowerment, and a committed partnership in everyone's success journey. Our approach is holistic and entails strategic services and case management plans to address the needs of the whole person, assessing and then providing support in all areas identified as contributing causes of homelessness.

To ensure adequate assessment and access to services, the LAM partners with other organizations to provide all residents admitted into the program with an initial behavioral health baseline assessment, one-on-one counseling services, and enrollment in continual telehealth psychoeducational classes and groups facilitated by the LAM's Educational Center. Class topics include addiction and relapse prevention, seeking peace, and a host of other behavioral health needs.

All individuals entering the program with a diagnosable mental health disorder receive medication evaluations and prescription refills via a partnership with a mental health service organization. Additionally, the Los Angeles Mission's Learning Resource Center hosts various academic and legal classes, career development, vocational training, and employment opportunities to address advancement in this area. We also offer access to arts, social enterprise, housing navigation, narcotics anonymous and alcoholics anonymous groups, relapse prevention, family reunification assistance, and the list goes on. We offer these as part of our commitment to walk alongside those we serve to provide resources, as well as a structured program and stable environment, for healing, reconciliation, recovery, and housing.

This is what holistic engagement on a services level can look like. And I see this succeed every day.

A Challenge and a Blessing

When it comes to working with people who need God's saving grace and healing, it takes the Word of God and the Holy Spirit to walk alongside those often stigmatized as the "poor, oppressed, and broken-hearted." Witnessing God's redemptive and transformative power manifested in people's lives has been humbling and awe-inspiring, and it has strengthened my faith. I have seen how when we engage the people who walk through our doors, God can truly be at work.

As you think about ways your church can engage homelessness on a practical level, I challenge you to be engaged personally and spiritually as well. Engage fully with the documentary, the study guide readings, the Scriptures, and other participants as active partakers in the Bible study.

I encourage you to engage in transparent self-reflection, introspection, and prayer in order to assess your own experiences, perceptions, denial, fears, or biases about homelessness and people experiencing homelessness. In the safety and presence of God with fellow believers, share your hearts, attitudes, beliefs, and feelings toward those who are deemed the "poor, needy, or marginalized"—those who, on any given day of the year, find themselves a statistic, caught in the complex cycle of homelessness.

May you be engaged by the Lord in a new way to continue growing in knowledge, wisdom, faith, hope, and love out of a submitted heart in the power of His Spirit, and not merely as a work of the flesh, knowing that God is using your gifts, time, talents, and mental and intellectual capacity to move His agenda, promoting His kingdom on earth.

> "But with righteousness he will judge the needy, with justice he will give decisions for the poor of the earth."
> Isaiah 11:4

May the Holy Spirit endow you with an Isaiah 11–type of anointing that rests upon you and enables you (in a good way) to engage with wisdom, understanding, counsel, might, knowledge, and reverence to the Lord. That you won't feel coerced into anything by any false guilt, shame, or self-condemnation but instead actually act or engage out of a disposition of "delight in obeying the LORD." May the Holy Spirit endow you with the capacity to "not judge by appearance nor make a decision based on hearsay" (verse 3 NLT) but to be empowered to engage people, structures, industries, and systems for justice and equity in making fair decisions as opportunities present themselves for the cause of homelessness and those experiencing its adverse impacts in our nation (verse 4).

True Belonging

Rev. John Samaan

President and CEO of Boston Rescue Mission

Most of the people who become homeless and seek help at the Boston Rescue Mission have already hit "rock bottom"—that moment when all the problems and stress in their lives overwhelm them completely. Their lives are in crisis, and every crisis is interrelated. Understanding this is crucial to truly engage those who are experiencing homelessness rather than enable them.

Some come into homelessness by means of financial hardship, as the result of a change in a relationship, after struggling with mental illness, or through other circumstances one would never expect. Homelessness in many cases is the result of deeply rooted personal difficulties. The very euphemism "homeless" can be a misnomer; the provision of housing alone cures neither an addiction nor a mental illness. This misconception comes from the way some homelessness advocates have defined and labeled the issue since the 1980s. **By calling those with chronic addiction and mental illness who find themselves on our streets "homeless," it gives the impression that the common solution to their problems is simply to house them.**

The spiraling down and decomposition into the condition of homelessness is most often a very complex series of interconnected tragedies: untreated mental illness, self-medication to a point of addiction, loss of a job, inability to pay off credit cards and bills, loss of housing, loss of friends, shunning by family members, car repossession, then to the streets. It is important to understand that a single-solution approach to solving the complex challenges of homelessness will neither effectively recognize nor address the complex needs of this troubled population.

When we're talking about engaging versus enabling behaviors, housing may seem like it falls under the engagement category. But housing is complicated.

Housing is necessary and part of the solution as long as it is supported by appropriate treatment and accountability. Long-term solutions to the problem require using all the tools in our toolbox and a long-term commitment to the people we serve, an array of services, accountability, and genuine grace and compassion. To be successful, we need to engage people in treatment and have the patience to see them through to their recovery. Expecting a person who has been experiencing homelessness due to addiction for fifteen years to recover to self-sufficiency in fifteen days is unrealistic.

> # Expecting a person who has been experiencing homelessness due to addiction for fifteen years to recover to self-sufficiency in fifteen days is unrealistic.

For example, for someone who is experiencing homelessness due to addiction, consequences and accountability can be that person's salvation. People struggling with addiction will continue to indulge as long as they feel that the rewards of using outweigh the pain. It is important that a person demonstrate a sincere desire for sobriety when enrolling in a program and that they will be held to that commitment or incur the consequences. A long-lasting successful recovery from a chronic substance use addiction requires a commitment to a program for several hours a week for several months, followed with supervised accountability and aftercare. It requires courage, encouragement, and extensive participation in their own healing and others' as well.

In addition, evidence-based addiction treatment studies point to the importance of engaging participants in productive activities.[2] We have always encouraged participants in our longer-term programs to contribute what they can give to the benefit of the community. Part of the healing process at the Mission is found in humble service to others. We are all in the same circle of healing, and we have the responsibility to use our gifts to serve. Ralph Waldo Emerson said, "Every man I meet is my master in some point, and in that I learn of him."[3] Everyone has something to contribute. Everyone is needed. Everyone has something to teach.

Alcoholics Anonymous recognizes this principle by simply saying: "The only way to keep it is to give it away." Ironically, the accountability, healing, and care that are shared within a recovery community can reveal their own paths to healing in ways one might not expect.

Housing someone who is struggling with an addiction will not bring them to true healing and sobriety. It will more likely enable the addictive behavior, and frequently leads to death. While the steps I mentioned above take far more time, attention, and intentionality, they are what will fully engage an addict in a way that will help them find true and lasting healing.

Home and Belonging

From my thirty-five years of working and living among the people who experience homelessness, I have discovered that most of the issues they face come from a deeply rooted loneliness, rejection, brokenness, and lack of belonging.

I recall a conversation with a graduate from the Mission's recovery program as she described how the seduction of addiction made her feel "at home." She told me that when she was under the influence of drugs, she felt that she belonged, and her loneliness went away as long as she was high. But as most addicts know well, these moments progressively worsen as the addiction takes over the person and the loneliness and the void widen.

The majority of those with chronic addiction are unaffirmed people. Their core desperately needs healing through the gift of unconditional love. The greatest trap we may all face in our lives is self-rejection. When we come to believe the deceptive voices that call us worthless and unlovable, the destructive and addictive behaviors usually resurface. Self-rejection and societal rejection contradict the loving voice of God that calls us beloved children (Galatians 4:3–7).

The greatest trap we may all face in our lives is self-rejection.

> "So you are no longer a slave, but God's child; and since you are his child, God has made you also an heir."
> Galatians 4:7

Many of the women and men who we serve have their lives laid bare; they are pushed to the brink of destruction by addiction, abuse, poverty, and damaging life choices. When they break loose from these bonds, they are able to continue the long, humble road of healing. Their wounds are slowly transformed into reminders of their need for God, friends, and continuing growth.

In my view, no services will bring a lasting cure to chronic human pain unless they address the issues of acceptance and belonging. Safe and affordable housing for our society's unhoused is necessary, but I hope we can envision the place called "home" as a safe and loving place where we can belong. The power of home is in its sense of community, connection, and how it helps us to see ourselves as whole. It is a place of unlimited potential, a safe place where we allow ourselves to receive nourishment, healing, and an oasis of transformation.

At the Boston Rescue Mission, we do not believe that we have done our part by merely providing an emergency shelter bed and a hot meal, job, or housing to someone who is struggling with addiction or experiencing homelessness. In fact, this simply marks the beginning of a relationship of trust with our guests, where we can support them on their journey out of homelessness and into the courageous journey of self-awareness, belonging, recovery, and transformation.

The greatest need of most people is not for food, clothing, and housing. Rather, it is for unconditional love and belonging—to know that someone believes in them, that they belong in a supportive community where they can contribute in a meaningful way and have a relationship with the God of second chances, who fills our hearts and always offers us a new beginning. Only love, acceptance, and true belonging can heal.

The Dos and Don'ts of Church Engagement in Homelessness

Don't start a new non-profit. It is not helpful to duplicate services and add to administrative costs.

Do support and partner with existing successful ministries. Combining resources under one roof brings strength and effectiveness, instead of duplication of services.

Don't hand out food in the park or on the street. This is an enabling behavior.

Do help prepare and serve meals at a successful organization such as Citygate Network Rescue Mission or at a Salvation Army location.

Don't assume you have nothing to offer to those who are experiencing homelessness just because you have never worked with people experiencing homelessness before.

Do share your time, talent, and treasure, whatever it may be, in any amount. Every faith-based and non-profit organization providing homelessness services in the US can use additional talent, volunteers, and financial support. Faith-based services depend on gifts of time and talent, as well as financial generosity, in order to be successful. There is a wide array of volunteer opportunities where talents can be harvested.

Session 2 Group Guide
Welcome

Welcome to session 2's group guide of the *No Address Interactive Study Guide*. Before you get started in this week's session, take some time to reflect on your "go and do" action items from last week.

1. What did you learn about homelessness in your community?

2. What did you learn about Jesus?

3. What did you learn about yourself?

Watch

Hopefully you had a chance to read about engaging versus enabling from Dr. Roxanne Jordan and Rev. John Samaan, who talked about what enabling looks like, what true engagement looks like, and how we can act in a way that actually makes a difference for those experiencing homelessness on a practical and spiritual level.

> **Watch the Session 2 Intro video.**
> **(You can access the video via the QR code or link on page 36.)**

Discussion

Discuss what you just watched and the material you read this week using the following questions as a guide.

1. When in your life have you experienced true engagement from someone else, or when have you engaged with others? When have you been enabled by someone else, or when have you enabled someone?

2. What thoughts or feelings do you have after watching the Intro Video for this session? Which parts resonated with you, and why?

3. When have you engaged someone who was experiencing homelessness, if ever? When have you unknowingly enabled someone experiencing homelessness? How do these experiences compare to each other?

4. When or where do you feel most at home, and why? What kind of home does someone who is experiencing homelessness really need, and what could that look like?

What Does the Bible Say?

Read Mark 14:3–9.

1. In Mark 14:7, Jesus said, "The poor you will always have with you." What do you think He meant by this? If the poor will always be with us, should we continue to work to eradicate poverty and homelessness? Why, or why not?

2. Rather than selling her perfume to help the poor, the woman in this story poured it over Jesus's feet. What did this symbolize?

How could putting Jesus first in our lives help us serve others better, through engagement rather than enablement?

3. Read Galatians 4:1–7.

How did Jesus change our identity? How does this affect our sense of belonging?

4. How could this feeling of belonging transform the life of someone who is experiencing homelessness?

Go and Do

Watch the Session 2 Wrap-up video.
(You can access the video via the QR code or link on page 36.)

What can you do as a group and individually this week to apply what you learned about homelessness?

This week, **we** will:

This week, **I** will:

Pray

End your time by sharing prayer requests and praying for one another to feel equipped and encouraged to engage those who are experiencing homelessness. Record prayer requests below or in the journal pages at the end of the book, so you can continue to pray for one another throughout the week.

For Next Week

Read Session 3 on pages 79–90.

If you want to learn more about this week's topic, check out the following resource: John Samaan, *Parables to Live By* (Boston Rescue Mission, 2007).

Reflect

Use the questions below to reflect on your "go and do" action item this week.

1. Describe your "go and do" task for the week. What did you do? Who did you meet?

2. What did you learn about the state of homelessness in your community?

3. What did you learn about Jesus?

4. What did you learn about yourself?

The Importance of Partnering with Successful Service Agencies

Rev. Bob Gehman

President Emeritus of Helping Up Mission

Dr. Denis Antoine II

Director of the Center for Addiction, Johns Hopkins Bayview Medical Center

A Vision for Helping People Up

Rev. Bob Gehman

Illicit drug use and addiction, along with their devastating results, are not exclusively inner-city problems or ones that can be relegated as "their problem." Dependency on alcohol, as well as both illegal and legal drugs, is pervasive in all our communities throughout the US: in suburbs, in affluent and educated households, across workplaces, in community organizations, and even in our houses of worship. Unfortunately, this trapped group of people is growing exponentially, and at a great cost of human lives, human resources, dollars, and demoralization of our families and communities. In my three decades of experience working with this population, addiction is by far the principal cause of homelessness.

In Baltimore, our leaders have tried to brand the city as "Charm City." Paradoxically, it is a commonly accepted statistic that one out of ten of our city residents are "charmed" by an illicit drug-trafficker. Sadly, Baltimore has one of the highest per capita drug addiction rates in the country. Whenever we work to address a problem of this crisis proportion, it requires sufficient energy and resources, and at a level of sophistication that is equal to its complexity, its powerful lures, and its devastating impacts.

For the past thirty years, I have worked in the trenches at Helping Up Mission. Over that time, I have served tens of thousands of people experiencing homelessness who struggle with addiction, attempting to give them the opportunity to become free and to find a new and bright future. A future that helps put addiction in their rearview mirror.

It has always been my way of thinking that, in the city with some of the worst problems in the US, we need to respond by setting up the most successful and respected drug recovery program in the country.

That is what we set out to achieve at Helping Up Mission. In many ways we have accomplished the goal of transforming lives, but our work is far from over. We are challenged to keep advancing the programs to compete with the ever-evolving and more powerful drugs like fentanyl and the devastating animal sedative xylazine (known as "tranq" on the street) that are on our streets. I feel morally bound to share this hard-learned "helping up" model for recovery to others who are serious about making a difference in their communities.

Every city in our country needs something like Helping Up Mission (HUM) to provide help for people who are caught in the trap of addiction and homelessness. The flagship program at HUM is called our Spiritual Recovery Program. I believe the program is a model for addressing the problem of addiction holistically: meeting people where they are and giving them the hope and the drive for a better life.

Our highly successful program came from humble beginnings.

In 1994, HUM was providing emergency overnight guest services to approximately 150 men experiencing homelessness. Most of the men at our rescue mission were from the inner city. We offered the typical mission formula of an evening meal, chapel service, overnight lodging, breakfast, and then repeat. These "three hots and a cot" services were intended to provide the men with hope for the future. But as important as our work was, it was not working. Providing emergency basic needs was certainly the difference between life and death to those men, but it was not providing them with hope for a better future, not providing *recovery*.

We had to start thinking more deeply about what could be done to change our program outcomes. We observed that most men in our program were experiencing alcoholism, drug addiction, and mental illness. *This observation would be critical to our success, for it would define our mission going forward.* But we had to do more than superficially see this; we had to deeply understand its significance and be prepared to confront the truth that meeting the basic needs of food and shelter was not nearly enough.

Many people think that helping people up is a simple matter. It is not.

This is hard work that can be complicated and risky and seems to be *always* short of resources! Yet not helping is not an option. Our faith requires more. Our own mental and spiritual health and overall quality of life depend on each of us helping others in a productive and right manner. Our civil society and sense of community rest on the foundation of neighbors helping neighbors who need a helping hand.

Maybe the most important lesson we learned is that helping people means listening more. We could not tell people what they needed; instead, we needed to first ask, then listen, to our neighbors. When we asked the men sleeping in our shelter what they needed, they overwhelmingly told us about their addictions to drugs and alcohol. Over time we kept observing and listening. Then came the fundamental realization that untreated mental illness and trauma were at the root of the addiction problem.

As a result of our observations, we concluded if we did not offer programs that addressed addiction and untreated mental illness, we would remain an emergency operation with no long-term hope of our residents seeing a better future.

> # If we did not offer programs that addressed addiction and untreated mental illness, we would remain an emergency operation with no long-term hope of our residents seeing a better future.

Our Christian faith provided the daily energy to persevere over a lengthy period of time to find a new way of serving that would truly help people up and into recovery. In so many ways this work strengthened our own individual faiths. Whenever we've set our goals in alignment with God's plan, He has sent the people and resources to our mission to achieve those goals! He sent us a strong non-profit staff who found the best ways to help people. He sent us faithful volunteers who engaged in the helping process as well. He sent us partners and collaborators who brought their expertise and resources to bear. A commitment to personal and organizational growth helped us find the answers we needed to always take next steps.

We started our Spiritual Recovery Program (SRP) by asking ourselves a fundamental question: How does a person experiencing homelessness, addiction, and mental illness become healthy and have a bright future?

We also had two secondary questions: What would help our residents gain sobriety? What are the challenges and roadblocks in remaining sober?

After years of talking with and listening to thousands of residents, **we developed a program that truly provides men and women—who on average have twenty-plus years of addiction and thirty months of incarceration time—with the hope they need to transform their lives.**

Thousands of people have seized the opportunity and enrolled in our programs, and more importantly, thousands have succeeded in recovery. Success breeds success, and today, Helping Up Mission has five hundred men and a new Center for Women and Children with room for two hundred women and fifty children in active recovery.

What did we find to be most helpful for our residents to gain sobriety and life transformation? The answer can be boiled down to four strategic program ingredients:

- long-term
- full-time residential
- faith and spirituality at the forefront
- all treatment and supportive services under one roof

Long-Term Program

It is no surprise to fellow practitioners that the success of the SRP relies on the length of the program. After twenty-plus years of addiction that have led a person to homelessness, and all its destructive ingredients, change will not come easy or fast. By the time a resident arrives at our door, they are almost always in complete despair. Most have tried short-term programs but have failed repeatedly. It is unrealistic to expect a person with long-term addiction who has been living on the street for decades to recover in twenty-eight or even ninety days.

It is a miracle that there is still a flicker of hope left in these individuals to try another program. I am reminded of the poet Alexander Pope, who wrote, "He is the good man in whose breast Hope springs eternal."[1] It always amazes me when residents tell themselves that maybe this time it will work, and against the odds, they will give it one more try. Their eternal hope strengthens my own drive to not let them down.

Lessons like breaking the yearlong program into phases helped our residents experience milestone achievements throughout the year, which kept them motivated. And commemorating the completion of each phase with a celebration and presentation of certificates at our chapel allowed our residents to be even more motivated by their achievements.

Upon completion of all four program phases a diploma is presented, and the resident can publicly share a portion of their success story at the graduation ceremony, which offers hope to others. Family members and staff are all invited to participate in these celebrations of spiritual recovery and program success. I cannot underscore enough the importance of this step. We are serving a population for whom graduations, positive recognition, and applause are extremely rare; the pride of achieving each goal is foundational to their long-term success in recovery.

Not letting our residents down is no small challenge! The kind of change required to be successful is a comprehensive change in mind, body, and spirit. The human soul has extraordinary capacity to change, but it is a slow, one-day-at-a-time process with many difficulties along the way. It is the kind of change a twenty-eight-day short-term program cannot deliver, especially with the power of addiction and desire to use being so strong. Over time, many residents on their own have seen the value of staying even longer than one year to become stronger in their recovery foundation.

Full-Time Residential Recovery Community

The kind of life change that is required seldom happens alone. But most residents have destroyed their most important family and friend relationships, and have burned many bridges behind them. The power of the residential community encourages deep and meaningful life change. Living in a recovery community enhances the building of relationships, grows interpersonal skills, and provides constant feedback from the group conscience and program structure.

> # The kind of life change that is required seldom happens alone.

It is important to note that isolation from the rest of the world and deep-seated loneliness is a typical condition of most people experiencing homelessness and addiction. Living in a recovery community that feels like a supportive family provides opportunity for healthy socialization. This is a huge component in establishing a new quality of life.

Faith and Spirituality Are Key

Helping Up Mission is a Christian program with faith and spirituality as its lifeblood, because without faith, nothing else seems to work. Christ and the Bible, along with the twelve steps of recovery, which we believe support biblical teaching, are the heart and soul of the HUM residential community. These provide the values upon which we live our lives.

While our clients do not have to be religious or espouse the Christian faith to be in the SRP, many do. But most participate because, at a minimum, they desire the benefits of a faith environment while working on their recovery. Being surrounded by a faith culture, and the growing of an individual's faith, provides an atmosphere of hope that can keep progress alive in the face of great difficulty.

The spirituality of working the twelve steps opens the heart to an active life power beyond oneself. Combining faith with working the twelve steps leads many to experience a true dynamic relationship with God the Father, Son, and Holy Spirit. This experience brings staying power to the necessary daily work that keeps life transformation happening. In my view, informed by observing and conversing with thousands of addicted people over the past thirty years, faith and spirituality are essential in gaining sobriety and having a sustained quality of life beyond drugs. This is why faith and spirituality are foundational and central to all our program design and execution.

All Treatment and Supportive Services under One Roof

In order to focus on gaining sobriety and life change, providing the basic needs of the individual helps the resident be as stress-free as possible. We can have the best ideas for program outcomes, but if basic human needs are not addressed, all our good efforts will be lost. These include common-sense things like securing reading glasses, addressing tooth pain, offering primary medical care and behavioral health care, and providing balanced nutrition, to name a few.

Once we learned this to be true, and that we could not afford to hire all the professionals needed to perform these basic human services, we realized the necessity to significantly collaborate with strategic community partners. **Little can be accomplished when you work alone. The strength of an organization can be measured by the strength of its partner relationships.**

Learning to collaborate with reputable partners who have similar interests in supporting people experiencing homelessness and addiction was a real SRP breakthrough. Over time we have formalized these relationships through written agreements and memoranda of understanding. If it weren't for our partnerships with other service agencies, we likely wouldn't be able to meet everyone's basic human needs.

These partnerships directly help our residents, and they help our overall HUM organization become even stronger through cross-pollination of ideas, expertise, and resources. They make us better at what we do, and we have a similar effect on our partners.

It's critical to proactively manage all the appointments—connecting our residents with our partners in all areas of human need. When appointments happen, critical services can be delivered. If services are delivered consistently over time, people's lives are changed. It's typical to have approximately eight thousand monthly appointments that need management, so we've tapped into technology for a system that is easy to understand and use.

Every mission resident has a name tag and barcode. The clients simply scan their barcodes at kiosks located at key points throughout our mission to pull up their daily schedules. Residents then "swipe" into appointments, meetings, treatment sessions, as well as their work responsibilities. This system monitors attendance and creates accountability for fulfilling appointments. Attendance records are kept so case managers can monitor progress, and when needed, appropriate interventions can result when appointments are not kept.

Improvement Takes Dedication

These four programmatic ingredients took a lot of time to learn and fully develop. We continue to learn after almost three decades, constantly adjusting our programs to meet the evolving needs of our residents. It sounds simple, but the hard part is the practical implementation, which requires work, patience, and persistence on the part of talented, enthusiastic, solution-oriented staff who never give up and never stop growing in their knowledge, understanding, and experience. These same staff also must model the character required to gain sobriety and experience transformational recovery.

The program reached a new level of strength and success when after several years of implementation, graduates became staff members and offered leadership and help to newcomers. From their lived experiences of surviving on the street and then navigating the recovery program, they are able to give encouragement and improve the program through their innovative ideas. Input from graduates was a huge step in development and improvement!

Even though program development and improvement take time and patience, I truly believe Helping Up Mission's SRP can be replicated in other communities in a much shorter period of time by learning from our experiences.

Helping Up Mission's Baltimore location places it in the backyard of the world-renowned medical institution Johns Hopkins. Over time, Johns Hopkins University and Health System have become our strongest community partners with HUM, locating direct services and a clinic within our mission. Our partnership with Johns Hopkins is led by Dr. Denis Antoine II, a Johns Hopkins psychiatrist who leads a drug treatment and behavioral health program called Cornerstone. Through his visionary leadership, HUM has a Hopkins' behavioral health program embedded inside our mission. Dr. Antoine elaborates below about his partnership experiences and the benefits of strong community collaboration that would otherwise be insurmountable.

Johns Hopkins

Dr. Denis Antoine II

It is critically important to state that effective partnerships rely on the support of leadership at the highest levels. Without the support of leaders at Helping Up Mission such as Bob Gehman working closely with the leadership of Johns Hopkins University, this partnership would never have begun.

Partner building is hard work. And as we built the partnership between Johns Hopkins and the Helping Up Rescue Mission, we realized that success often proves to be much more nuanced than anything we can draft on paper.

Formal agreements between partners, such as memorandums of understanding, are critical to defining the operational, financial, and administrative needs of each institution. They represent and codify the commitment to a process that can be turbulent in its quest for excellence. These documents also serve as a set of grounding principles when the partnership becomes turbulent.

Why turbulent? Because as you seek to build partnerships in the present, the complicated past history of the institutions can reemerge. For example, many academic institutions, such as Johns Hopkins, are still earning the trust of the community due to past ethical breaches that have either under-resourced, overlooked, or sometimes directly harmed underserved populations. Likewise, some community partners have a history of thinking they would not benefit from large university involvement. This could have doomed our partnership from the start.

Being "the expert" on behavioral health treatment was not enough to overcome this history. In fact, larger academic institutions, with their "ivory towers," at times can come across as knowing more than the community-based partner, thus devaluing the views of the community partner.

It became clear to us in building the partnership between HUM and Hopkins that we needed to rescript the typical outcomes of this type of partnership.

Our partnership needed to be built on trust. The key model of trust that I have remained focused on comprises four key elements:

- consistency
- reliability
- intimacy
- self-orientation

While consistency and reliability are similar in nature, there are nuances that should be considered when engaging a partnership. It could be easy enough for each institution to work independently in parallel. However, doing so decreases communication and the chances for joint problem solving. To overcome these issues, we felt there was a need for regular meetings among staff members from both institutions for timely discussion of roadblocks or misunderstandings that arose. The need for these meetings was easily accepted by parties in both institutions. Many of these meetings are still happening on a weekly basis eleven years into our partnership.

The need for reliability became clear early in the process. Johns Hopkins provided an evidence-based treatment program but had struggled with coordinating the services being offered to people experiencing homelessness, thus not benefiting from the strengths of Helping Up Mission. Recognizing mutual strengths of the partners combined with regular communication improved treatment for the residents.

Prior to the start of our consistent and structured meetings, HUM residents attended only 30 to 40 percent of scheduled services. After system improvements were put in place, the residents maintained an attendance rate of over 80 percent, even at the height of the COVID-19 pandemic. Successfully navigating treatment services while social-distancing requirements were in place demonstrates that this model can overcome even the most significant barriers.

Our continued rate of services during the COVID-19 pandemic illuminates the importance of the other two principles of trust: intimacy and self-orientation. Through a deep understanding of each other's day-to-day operations, a partnership can withstand threats to its sustainability.

It would be quite easy for an institution like Johns Hopkins to solely focus on its own mission of research or other university-driven endeavors. Instead, it has been critical that we also consider the needs, risks, and values of Helping Up Mission and create an atmosphere of transparent decision making, and vice versa. We have reached more people in need of services by working together. We now have enrolled nearly two thousand residents since the Johns Hopkins clinic's opening at Helping Up Mission.

The glue for our partnership has been an ambassador from each institution who can effectively lead and shepherd communication, especially during turbulent times in the partnership. I was the ambassador from Johns Hopkins, which meant that I often had to represent the message of Helping Up Mission to my colleagues who didn't have intimate knowledge. Likewise, our partnership has benefited from multiple individuals from Helping Up Mission who have played a similar role in reverse.

The goal was to increase efficiencies by taking an existing Johns Hopkins service and placing it inside of HUM. Johns Hopkins certainly had the reputation for delivering high-quality care within the walls of our institution. By applying the principles presented above and working in partnership, we have been able to cross the chasm that initially existed and deliver truly world-class care to people who had previously experienced homelessness.

These "four principles of trust" can be applied as a formula to almost all partnerships. The Helping Up Mission and Johns Hopkins partnership is now a nationally recognized success. We hope these lessons will guide you as you look to form your own partnerships.

Session 3 Group Guide
Welcome

Welcome to session 3's group guide of the *No Address Interactive Study Guide*. Before you get started in this week's session, take some time to reflect on your "go and do" action items from last week.

1. What did you learn about homelessness in your community?

2. What did you learn about Jesus?

3. What did you learn about yourself?

Watch

Hopefully you had a chance to read about joining with established partnerships from Rev. Bob Gehman and Dr. Denis Antoine II, who talked about the difference it makes on a practical and spiritual level.

> **Watch the Session 3 Intro video.**
> **(You can access the video via the QR code or link on page 36.)**

Discussion

Discuss what you just watched and the material you read this week using the following questions as a guide.

1. Have you or a loved one ever struggled with addiction or undiagnosed mental health issues? Have you ever sought to help someone struggling with these things?

2. What thoughts or feelings do you have after watching Rev. Gehman's and Dr. Antoine's interviews? Which parts resonated with you, and why?

3. When have you considered what partnerships are available in your community to help address the issues of addiction and homelessness, if ever?

4. In what ways do you now feel better informed about helping someone struggling with addiction, mental health issues, or homelessness? What kind of service does someone who is experiencing homelessness really need, and what could that look like?

What Does the Bible Say?

Read Ecclesiastes 4:9–12.

1. In verse 9, the teacher said, "Two are better than one, because they have a good return for their labor." How do you think this applies to the type of partnership described in this session?

2. Sometimes a partnership can get messy, as Dr. Antoine described. But even so, this Scripture passage describes the benefits of partnering with others. In what ways can partnership be a blessing, even in its more challenging moments?

3. Read 1 Peter 5:8–11.
Why did Peter encourage the believers to remain sober and vigilant? How might teaching others to resist the devil aid in addiction recovery?

4. How might someone struggling with addiction be empowered to know that God will restore them and make them strong, in His power?

Go and Do

Watch the Session 3 Wrap-up video.
(You can access the video via the QR code or link on page 36.)

What can you do as a group and individually this week to apply what you learned about homelessness?
This week, **we** will:

This week, **I** will:

Pray

End your time by sharing prayer requests and praying for one another to feel equipped and encouraged to engage those who are experiencing homelessness. Record prayer requests below or in the journal pages at the end of the book, so you can continue to pray for one another throughout the week.

For Next Week

Read Session 4 on pages 95–104.

Reflect

Use the questions below to reflect on your "go and do" action item this week.

1. Describe your "go and do" task for the week. What did you do? Who did you meet?

2. What did you learn about the state of homelessness in your community?

3. What did you learn about Jesus?

4. What did you learn about yourself?

Session 4

Yes, *You* Can Help

Commissioner Jolene Hodder

The Salvation Army National Headquarters

What *You* Can Do

My husband and I were taking part in the Grate Patrol, which we do often in our roles with The Salvation Army. The Grate Patrol is a program that takes its name from the heating grates in Washington DC, where the homeless community congregates, especially on cold winter days. For decades, The Salvation Army has been going to homeless encampments in the nation's capital *every* night of the year, regardless of how bad the weather is, serving meals, offering hope, and engaging people to come into shelter and treatment programs.

It was bitterly cold that night, and few were willing to come out of their makeshift shelters. So, we called out to tell them that The Salvation Army was there.

One tent in particular caught my eye. It was surrounded by a waist-high fence made of cardboard that had been whitewashed and decorated with plastic flowers. As I walked around it, I discovered a creatively designed gate. Behind that gate was a little yard with a small table and chair. Displayed on the table were mismatched plates, napkins, utensils, and a small Bible, which had been propped up as a centerpiece. As I opened the gate, a middle-aged woman crawled out of the tent and welcomed me. When I told her how much I admired her decorations, she seemed to stand a bit taller. And when I told her I particularly liked the Bible, she beamed! She pulled down her COVID mask and said, "God has been so good to me." I nodded and asked if she wanted something to eat. She followed me to The Salvation Army canteen, ate several bowls of soup, filled her pockets with other foodstuffs, and then asked me if she could help serve others.

As I watched her graciously serve her neighbors who were experiencing homelessness that evening, I was reminded of 1 Peter 4:10, "Each of you should use whatever gift you have received to serve others, as faithful stewards of God's grace in its various forms."

Time, Talent, and Treasure
When it comes to how you as an individual can help with the homelessness crisis, start small by thinking about your time, talent, and treasure—offering these to existing service agencies and shelters is a great way to start.

Time: This can be any amount of time that you have, from twenty minutes a week to two hours to a full day. Every season of life is different. How much time can you realistically devote now to volunteering or helping in some way?	Talent: You may think you don't have what it takes to serve those who are experiencing homelessness, but all skills are valuable in this line of work. What skills do you already have? Writing? Cooking? Welcoming others? Organizing events? Professional services? Existing service agencies need help of all kinds. Think outside the box. What talent could you offer to help?	Treasure: Of course, financial help is always needed, and in the non-profit world, it is often scarce. You don't have to donate large sums. Whatever you can share is always helpful. When you are short on time, this can be a great way to contribute.

On any given night, roughly 600,000 Americans are experiencing "street-level, unsheltered" homelessness.[1] Many individuals want to do something to help, but sometimes the problem seems so overwhelming, potential volunteers do not know where to begin. It seems hopeless to many. **The good news is that anyone can serve, and everyone can make a difference.**

Pray for Guidance

Jonathan Edwards wrote, "There is no way that Christians in a private capacity can do so much to promote the work of God, and advance the kingdom of Christ, as by prayer."[2]

James 1:5 says, "If any of you lacks wisdom, you should ask God, who gives generously to all without finding fault, and it will be given to you." When we pray for God's guidance and leading through the Holy Spirit, we can be assured that God will show us what to do and how to do it, and He will equip us for that calling. We do not have to worry about our next step. We simply need to let Him direct us.

Prayer for Wisdom and Discernment

Dear Heavenly Father, open my eyes and help me to see those in need in my community. Jesus, help me see Your face in the eyes of every homeless person I meet. I pray for all women and men, boys and girls who do not have homes. For those sleeping in doorways and parks, in hostels and night shelters. For families who were evicted because they couldn't pay their rent. For those who have no relatives or friends who can take them in. For those who are afraid and without hope. Give me a heart of compassion and show me what I can do to serve those who have no place they call home. Use me, Lord, as You will. In Jesus's name, amen.

Practice the Best Type of Engagement: Kindness

Sometimes the simplest gestures can be the most impactful. One year my husband and I, along with representatives from other non-profits, were invited to the White House to view the Christmas decorations. It took awhile to go through the security protocols, so we waited in line outside of the White House, donned in our best attire. For us that meant our formal Salvation Army uniforms. During our wait, my husband greeted a man named Ron who was experiencing homelessness and walking by the White House. The man stopped, returned our smiles, and walked over to greet us. We asked his name and had a lovely extended conversation. As we stood visiting with this man, those in the line immediately around us moved away. Ron did not seem to notice. He just wanted to hear his name and be treated like a gentleman. He walked away with his head held high and a huge smile across his face, and never asked us for anything.

Homelessness often brings a sense of loneliness that can erode a person's self-worth. Unfortunately, many people who experience homelessness have grown accustomed to being ignored, looked down on, or treated with disrespect.

A simple smile can be very engaging, and looking into a person's eye sometimes breaks down years of distrust. Treat everyone with dignity and respect (as you would like to be treated).

As you do this, always be careful. Never place yourself in a dangerous situation. Remember that Jesus sent His disciples out in groups of two (Mark 6:7). Never go to an isolated or dark place alone; instead, work in teams of two or three. Do not wear expensive jewelry or carry a purse, and do not share personal information other than your name. Sometimes desperate people do desperate things; therefore, do not place yourself or them in a compromising position. Begin by simply acknowledging the people you encounter. Smile, greet them as you would at church, introduce yourself, ask their name, and begin a simple conversation. If the person indicates either verbally or with their body language that they are not interested in talking, respect their wishes and disengage.

Build Relationships

If the person is open to conversation, ask unintrusive questions, show interest, and actively listen. Many of our neighbors experiencing homelessness are also experiencing loneliness and crave conversation, and something as simple as a friendly exchange can make a huge difference.

Never wake someone who is sleeping and never make them feel trapped by approaching them in a large group or hovering over them where they are sitting on the ground or sidewalk. Always ask for permission before kneeling or sitting down next to someone.

As stated earlier, it is usually not a good idea to give money directly to a person experiencing homelessness. Many of the individuals experiencing homelessness have addictions, and many drugs are cheap and readily available. Therefore, instead of giving out money, keep a stock of nonperishable foods and bottled water in your car. The snack boxes like the ones served on airplanes are perfect to keep in your car for such occasions. Or offer to pick up something at their favorite fast-food restaurant. Perhaps you can even join them in a dining experience on the side of the road.

If you plan to distribute toiletries, do not assume people need packets of toiletries. Ask first what is needed. Often, they will pull out the items they need and throw away the rest. Do not give away new expensive clothing or equipment. Often these things will be sold for drugs and/or will be stolen, possibly endangering the life of the recipient.

It can be very engaging to have fellowship while you are sharing a meal. Conversations can build trust, which in turn presents opportunities of engagement that can lead to people exiting the street and hopefully joining a treatment program or entering a homeless assistance center. Likewise, if you just hand out food *without interaction and engagement*, it can be negatively enabling.

Do what you can to learn their story. It may take time to get to know someone, to build a relationship, but it is well worth it. Yes, you can do something to help someone during a onetime encounter. However, it takes time to discover the real cause of their plight. It takes time to discover why they are on the street and not in a shelter.

Steve and His Dog

It took almost a year to understand why Steve, a homeless veteran, would not come to our Salvation Army shelter. He seemed the perfect candidate for our housing program. After countless conversations, we finally built up enough trust for him to share that he would not go anywhere without his German Shepherd, the only family he had left in the world. We made some phone calls and arranged for him to stay at one of our shelters that had a pet program. A local veterinarian volunteering at the facility groomed the dog, performed a full examination, and administered the dog's shots. A local pet store provided a new collar and other supplies. The dog was allowed to sleep in a large pet cage next to Steve. That was the day Steve started his journey home.

Many men and women experiencing homelessness have heard about or experienced difficulties themselves with shelters in the past. Some concerns are real, and others are just perceived. The hesitation may be fear of shelter restrictions or theft of their few possessions, etc. By developing trust, and by partnering with a local homeless assistance center, you can help them navigate through their fears.

We must never assume we have the answers to the struggles of others. Only by learning their stories, listening without judging, and following the leading of the Holy Spirit will we be truly effective in getting our neighbors off the street.

All Hands on Deck

In serving God and His people, our role is to provide compassionate care without judgment. We do not know what trauma people have experienced, how it is currently affecting them, or what their current capacities are to find new ways to cope and survive.

When serving people experiencing homelessness, it is our greatest aim to help them to be in as safe a place as possible, both in the short-term as well as over a sustained period of time. We should work to provide opportunities for healing and movement toward self-sufficiency. We must strive to meet people where they are in their journey and serve them according to their own unique needs.

Continuing Christ's ministry is a hard and never-ending task. Reducing homelessness is an all-hands-on-deck effort, and each person can play a role. Building the public will to dramatically reduce homelessness is a key part of the challenge. Collectively, and with appropriate resources, we can prevent and reduce homelessness.

Helping Others through Wisdom and Discernment

Rev. Ron Brown

Associate Minister of Antioch Missionary Baptist Church

After leaving Haven for Hope as its director of outreach, I became a community engagement officer with the San Antonio Police Department (SAPD) and am blessed to report directly to the Police Chief. In this role, I often come across people experiencing homelessness, many of whom I have known for years.

Recently, I came across three friends over a span of four hours that focused my thinking on enabling versus engaging activities, and how to help people on an individual level in healthy ways.

As I was driving around for my job with SAPD, I happened upon one of my dearest friends, Jay. Jay had been living on and off the streets for years. He once had a promising career in football but had since turned to using drugs to cope with the challenges of living on the street. As I got out of my car to greet him, he was in his wheelchair happy to see me. He had a big smile on his face and a twinkle in his eyes. He said, "I am so proud of you, Ron Brown, and where you are in your life." I graciously smiled and thanked him.

The lower part of his leg had been amputated and was dirty and likely infected. I was saddened to see him in this condition. Jay began sharing with me his desire to get into a shelter where he could find help to take care of his needs. He asked me if I could connect him with a program, and I said yes. Then, before I walked away, he asked, "Do you have any money you can spare?" I dreaded hearing those words because I knew of his ongoing struggle with addiction. Knowing him, I knew where he would go and what he would do with the cash that I might give him. As hard as it was to do, I did not give him any money; instead, I assured him that I would connect him with our local homelessness assistance center.

Shortly after leaving Jay, on my way home, I went to a grocery store to pick up some items for dinner, when I ran into another friend, Ms. Sherry and her five kids. A fellow clergyman was talking to her and her family at the bus stop in the parking lot. They were waiting to get on a bus to head home after also visiting the grocery store.

The same question came up: "Do you have money that I can use for the bus?" This hit me harder because of her five children. She recently had secured housing, so she was not needing help with that. Unfortunately, Ms. Sherry did have a substance use disorder and struggled with addiction. Instead of giving her money, I offered to directly help buy her bus tickets for her family, and I gave her my business card. I also told her and her kids that I would be praying for them.

A few minutes later, I saw a longtime friend named Wanda. This was my third encounter on the same day with a friend who was struggling with homelessness. While I was getting a bag of ice outside the grocery store, I noticed her familiar face sitting in a car. I walked up to the car, and out jumped Wanda, merely skin and bones. She engulfed me with a hug, and I began to pray over her. She wept in my arms, saying she did not want me to see her like this.

I do not judge the appearance of people; I just love folks like they are. But I was worried about her. She was malnourished, and she was embarrassed to be seen. Before I had approached her, she had been waiting for me to leave the parking lot so she could discreetly go into the grocery store to buy food.

As I finished praying for her, I invited her to come to worship with me on Sundays, and to come as she was. Before I left to go back to my car, I asked her three times if she was okay or needed help. She shrugged off my questioning two times, then just like Jay and Ms. Sherry, she asked for money. She said if she could have one dollar, she could buy another item to eat. Wanda was clearly in a different position than my other two friends. She had been sitting in her car waiting for me to leave, hoping I would not see her. She needed help, and even though I asked her, she kept saying she was fine, but I could see she was not. God had put it on my heart to help her, so I did. I gave her several dollars and offered to help more, but she was embarrassed and did not want more.

Specific Circumstances Matter

The specific circumstances matter and are always unique. **Sometimes helping is enabling, and sometimes helping is lifesaving. It is important to discern the difference.** God is in control of everything. When the Holy Spirit speaks to our hearts and our minds, we need to listen.

Locate Resources in Your Area

I am always being asked "Where can I get help?" and "Where can I volunteer?"

In most communities, there are many faith-based and non-profit agencies providing services, and a listing of these services and organizations has already been compiled for a brochure or website. These lists are often put together by the United Way, the police department, or a city information line. If a comprehensive list already exists, use it, and do not reinvent the wheel. Likewise, if a comprehensive listing of services does not exist, consider compiling one.

Once you have a list of services and organizations, reach out to successful organizations to learn more about what they do. Learn how to refer families and individuals in need to these organizations and programs. Find out if these programs need volunteers and financial support (I am sure they could use the help and support). Learn how you can help an organization become a better organization.

Donate, Volunteer, and Support Local Community Leaders

As the old proverb goes, "One man's trash is another man's treasure." Donating items, giving financial support, and volunteering at homelessness assistance centers will make programs better and allow organizations to help more people.

Giving your time, talent, and treasure directly to established, successful organizations are the three best things you can do to help people experiencing homelessness. Directly help organizations that are already doing important things, and do not set up a new organization that competes with an existing organization. We do not need competition between groups; we need cooperation within God's kingdom.

We do not need competition between groups; we need cooperation within God's kingdom.

It is also important to support thoughtful community leaders who are working to reduce homelessness. You can help them in what they do by praying for them and becoming their eyes, legs, and hands. Help them become better at what they are doing in the community.

The Bible says, "In everything I did, I showed you that by this kind of hard work we must help the weak, remembering the words the Lord Jesus himself said: **'It is more blessed to give than to receive'**" (Acts 20:35). With a giving heart for the community of homelessness, support good leaders and hold all public officials accountable for the promises they make on this important issue. Use your voice as a voter to support policies that will truly reduce homelessness.

Session 4 Group Guide
Welcome

Welcome to session 4's group guide of the *No Address Interactive Study Guide*. Before you get started in this week's session, take some time to reflect on your "go and do" action items from last week.

1. What did you learn about homelessness in your community?

2. What did you learn about Jesus?

3. What did you learn about yourself?

Watch

This week, you read about how the individual can engage those who are experiencing homelessness with wisdom and discernment.

> **Watch the Session 4 Intro video.**
> **(You can access the video via the QR code or link on page 36.)**

Discussion

Discuss what you just watched and the material you read this week using the following questions as a guide.

1. When you think about what you, as an individual, can do to help homelessness, how do you feel? Why do you feel this way?

2. What thoughts or feelings do you have after watching the Session 4 Intro video? Which parts resonated with you, and why?

3. The leaders featured in the video offered several pieces of advice for how individuals can engage homelessness. What advice did you find the most helpful, and why? Did any of their advice surprise you? If so what, and why?

4. What do you feel most willing to give today: time, talent, or treasure? How could you give one of these to an existing service agency in your community?

What Does the Bible Say?

Read 1 Corinthians 12:12–27 and 1 Peter 4:8–10.

1. According to 1 Corinthians 12:12–27, how is the body a metaphor for the church? How have you experienced the church in this way?

How can this passage inform the way we approach homelessness as individuals who are parts of the greater body?

2. What gift do you believe you have received that you can use to help others? How have you seen this gift play out in your life? How could you use it to engage homelessness in your community?

> "So also faith by itself, if it does not have works, is dead."
> James 2:17

3. Read James 1:5; 3:13–18. According to these passages, how do we receive wisdom? What is wisdom, and what is it not?

4. How could you use godly wisdom in your daily encounters with those who are experiencing homelessness? Why is wisdom and discernment so important for these interactions?

Go and Do

Watch the Session 4 Wrap-up video.
(You can access the video via the QR code or link on page 36.)

What can you do as a group and individually this week to apply what you learned about homelessness?

This week, **we** will:

This week, **I** will:

Pray

End your time by sharing prayer requests and praying for one another to feel equipped and encouraged to engage those who are experiencing homelessness. Record prayer requests below or in the journal pages at the end of the book, so you can continue to pray for one another even as your study time together has come to an end.

If you want to learn more about this week's topic, check out the following resources:

- Kevin Nye, *Grace Can Lead Us Home: A Christian Call to End Homelessness* (Harrisonburg, VA: Herald Press, 2022).

- Elliot Liebow, *Tell Them Who I Am: The Lives of Homeless Women* (New York: Free Press, 1993).
- John W. Conrad, *To the Least of These: A Better Christian Response to Homelessness* (n.p., 2017).
- Derek Clark, song about life of a homeless man, GodTube, accessed October 30, 2023, www.godtube.com/watch/?v=YDZKPPNX.
- Share Change, The Salvation Army, "Homelessness Is Not a Life Sentence. It's a Circumstance," YouTube, posted October 28, 2022, www.youtube.com /watch?v=JdVmeqODAP0.

A call to action from St. Teresa of Ávila (1515–1582):

Christ has no body now but yours.
No hands, no feet on earth but yours.
Yours are the eyes through which he looks with compassion on this world.
Yours are the feet with which he walks to do good.
Yours are the hands through which he blesses all the world.
Yours are the hands, yours are the feet, yours are the eyes, you are his body.
Christ has no body now on earth but yours.

Reflect

Use the questions below to reflect on your "go and do" action item this week.

1. Describe your final "go and do" task. What did you do? Who did you meet?

2. What did you learn about the state of homelessness in your community?

3. What did you learn about Jesus?

4. What did you learn about yourself?

What Now?

Thank you for being interested in the homelessness issue, and for caring for the adults and families with children who are experiencing homelessness. Our *No Address* team appreciates you taking your valuable time to go through this study guide. We hope this was both informative and clarifying about the critical issues of homelessness.

Going forward, we hope you will thoughtfully engage with and share your love with the people you encounter who are experiencing homelessness. As in any relationship, dignity and respect will go a long way.

As you and your congregation become more involved in the issue of homelessness, we hope you will come alongside successful well-run organizations. Helping effective service agencies is by far the best way to directly help people experiencing homelessness. Supporting these organizations with your time, talent, and treasure will make all the difference in the world.

If you live in or work in an area where no or few organizations exist—a region that has true gaps in homelessness services—we hope you will collaboratively work with other caring people and congregations to fill those gaps in services.

Finally, we hope you will pursue efforts, individually and collectively, to actively engage people onto a pathway to exit homelessness, to become self-sufficient, and to avoid enabling activities that make the condition of homelessness worse.

We encourage you to get involved and to continue learning through other *No Address* resources (www.NoAddressMovie.com).

Homelessness affects all of us in so many ways. Please feel free to reach out to any of our *No Address* contributors, as shown on the following pages.

Thank you!

Dr. Robert G. Marbut Jr.
MarbutR@aol.com

No Address Contributors

Dr. Denis Antoine II serves as the director of Johns Hopkins Bayview Medical Center's Cornerstone Clinic, which provides addiction treatment services on-site at the Helping Up Mission in Baltimore, Maryland. These programs at the Cornerstone Clinic help underserved populations with substance use disorders and co-occurring mental health conditions. He is board-certified in psychiatry and addiction medicine and obtained his medical degree from Howard University, then completed his psychiatry residency at The Johns Hopkins Hospital, and went on to complete an NIH-sponsored addiction research fellowship at the Behavioral Pharmacology Research Unit on the Johns Hopkins Bayview campus.

John Ashmen served for sixteen years as the President of Citygate Network, North America's oldest and largest association of faith-focused crisis shelters and life-transformation centers. He has been an outspoken advocate for hungry, homeless, abused, and addicted people, and has addressed concerns and solutions in multiple mediums throughout the public and private sectors. John is the author of *Invisible Neighbors*, touted as the how-to manual for Christians serious about engaging with the poor and powerless.

 **Rev. Ronald K. Brown** is an associate minister at Antioch Missionary Baptist Church in San Antonio, Texas, and the community engagement officer for the San Antonio Police Department (SAPD). As the former outreach director for Haven for Hope, Rev. Brown has a heart for those experiencing homelessness. Through his work with the SAPD, he continues to interact daily with those experiencing homelessness, ministering to them and connecting them to crucial services.

Barbara Duffield is Executive Director of SchoolHouse Connection, a national non-profit organization working to overcome homelessness through education. For more than twenty years, she has bridged policy and practice in early care, education, housing, and homelessness. She received her bachelor's degree summa cum laude in Political Science from the University of Michigan.

Rev. Robert Gehman is President Emeritus of Helping Up Mission located in Baltimore, Maryland. During his twenty-nine years as CEO of Helping Up Mission, Rev. Gehman led the development of the long-term residential Spiritual Recovery Programs (SRP). Rev. Gehman has a master's degree in religious education (MRE) from Liberty University and has completed his graduate certification in non-profit studies at Johns Hopkins University. He also has his CFRE fundraising designation.

Commissioner Jolene Hodder is a Salvation Army officer with a passion for leading women to Christ and then equipping, motivating, and preparing them for effective ministry. She is the author of three published books, *A Bend in the Road*, *Walking in White*, and *Sensational Grace*. She was a 2021 recipient of the She Leads America award. Jolene has served in

the Army's Western Territory, Southern Territory, as well as International Headquarters, and eight years in Kenya. She currently ministers as the USA Salvation Army's National Secretary for Program. Jolene is the proud mother of one daughter, Jessica, who is married to her wonderful son-in-law, Tyler, and she adores spending time with her wonderful grandsons Everett and Oliver. Learn more at www.salvationarmyusa.org/usn/.

Dr. Roxanne Jordan is an advocate, educator, and leader in the field of mental health, addiction, and faith. She is committed to making a difference in the lives of those impacted by homelessness and trauma with a desire to decrease the stigma often associated with homelessness and mental health challenges while increasing literacy in these areas during our current world affairs. Her current mission is to improve the mental health and wellness of underserved segments of the population through community engagement, health education, counseling, and research.

Dr. Robert G. Marbut Jr. has worked on issues of homelessness for more than three decades, including being the Founding President and CEO of Haven for Hope and serving as the White House's "Federal Homelessness Czar." Dr. Marbut has consulted on issues of homelessness with more communities and organizations than anyone else in the United States and has also worked in three different US Presidential Administrations. He is an Executive Producer of both the *No Address* movie, starring Ashanti, Billy Baldwin, Xander Berkeley, and Beverly D'Angelo, as well as the *Americans with No Address* documentary. Dr. Marbut currently serves as a Senior Fellow at the Discovery Institute. Learn more at www.MarbutConsulting.org or contact at MarbutR@aol.com.

Rev. John Samaan was born and raised in Alexandria, Egypt. He began serving among the poor as a teenager by visiting families in the slums of Alexandria. For forty years he has been involved in organizations that serve the poor, both in the United States and abroad. For the last thirty-four years, he served among the homeless in Skid Row Los Angeles and in Boston, Massachusetts. John is the President of the Boston Rescue Mission. www.brm.org/mission-leadership. John authored *Parables to Live By* (Boston Rescue Mission, 2007).

Rev. Brandan Thomas is a pastor, advocate, and visionary leader based in Winchester, Virginia. With personal experience witnessing the impact of mental illness on his father, he possesses a deep understanding of homelessness and the challenges faced by individuals battling conditions such as schizophrenia and bipolar. As a husband, father, church planter,  and the CEO of the Winchester Rescue Mission, Thomas works toward creating transformative change in the lives of those in need, empowering communities, and fostering hope for a brighter future.

Notes

Introduction

1. US Department of Housing and Urban Development, *HUD Exchange*, "Category 1: Literally Homeless," accessed August 31, 2022, www.hudexchange.info/homelessness-assistance/coc-esg-virtual-binders/coc-esg-homeless-eligibility/four-categories/category-1/. US Department of Housing and Urban Development, "2020 AHAR: Part 1 - PIT Estimates." US Department of Education, National Center on Homeless Education, "Data and Statistics on Homelessness," accessed August 31, 2022, https://nche.ed.gov/data-and-stats/.

Glossary

1. Thank you to the Discovery Institute for allowing us to adapt some of their work into the development of this glossary.

Session 1

1. Janey Rountree, Nathan Hess, and Austin Lyke, "Health Conditions among Unsheltered Adults in the US," California Policy Lab, October 2019, www.capolicylab.org/wp-content/uploads/2023/02/Health-Conditions-Among-Unsheltered-Adults-in-the-U.S..pdf, 4–5.

2. Some names, including this one, have been changed to protect privacy.

3. Abraham Maslow's Hierarchy of Needs, as noted by Saul Mcleod, Simply Psychology, October 24, 2023, www.simplypsychology.org/maslow.html.

4. HUD Exchange, "Category 1: Literally Homeless," accessed October 29, 2023, www.hudexchange.info/homelessness-assistance/coc-esg-virtual-binders/coc-esg-homeless-eligibility/four-categories/category-1/.

5. US Department of Housing and Urban Development, *HUD Exchange*, "Category 1: Literally Homeless," accessed August 31, 2022, www.hudexchange.info/homelessness-assistance/coc-esg-virtual-binders/coc-esg-homeless-eligibility/four-categories/category-1/. US Department of Housing and Urban Development, "2020

AHAR: Part 1 - PIT Estimates of Homelessness in the U.S./2007-2020 Point-in-Time Estimates by State," accessed August 31, 2022, https://www.huduser.gov/portal/datasets/ahar/2020-ahar-part-1-pit-estimates-of-homelessness-in-the-us.html. US Department of Housing and Urban Development, "2020 AHAR: Part 1 - PIT Estimates of Homelessness in the U.S./2007-2020 Point-in-Time Estimates by State," accessed August 31, 2022, www.huduser.gov/portal/datasets/ahar/2020-ahar-part-1-pit-estimates-of-homelessness-in-the-us.html.

6. United States Drug Enforcement Administration, "Fentanyl," accessed October 29, 2023, www.dea.gov/factsheets/fentanyl#:~:text=Fentanyl%20is%20a%20potent%20synthetic,than%20heroin%20as%20an%20analgesic.

7. Health.am, "Homeless Alcoholics Typically Began Drinking as Children," June 27, 2014, www.health.am/psy/more/homeless-alcoholics-typically-began-drinking/#ixzz8E04W07vL.

8. National Center for Homeless Education, *Student Homelessness in America: School Years 2018–19 to 2020–21* (2022): https://nche.ed.gov/wp-content/uploads/2022/11/Student-Homelessness-in-America-2022.pdf, 4. "Annual Federal Data Summary School Years 2017–2018, Education for Homeless Children and Youth," Washington, DC: US Department of Education, https://nche.ed.gov/data-and-stats/.

9. Matthew Morton, et al., "Voices of Youth Count," Chapin Hall at the University of Chicago, accessed October 29, 2023, www.chapinhall.org/project/voices-of-youth-count/.

10. Barbara Duffield, "Reimagining Homelessness Assistance for Children and Families," *Journal of Children and Poverty*, September 1, 2020, DOI: 10.1080/10796126.2020.1813535.

11. Duffield, "Reimagining Homelessness," DOI: 10.1080/10796126.2020.1813535.

12. National Center for Homeless Education, *Student Homelessness in America,* https://nche.ed.gov/wp-content/uploads/2022/11/Student-Homelessness-in-America-2022.pdf, 8.

13. American Bar Association and SchoolHouse Connection, *Educating Students Experiencing Homelessness, Fifth Edition* (Washington, DC: ABA Book Publishing, 2018).

Session 2

1. Dictionary.com, s.v. "enable," accessed October 29, 2023, www.dictionary.com/browse/enable.

2. Ardú Recovery, "Support System: Support a Life in Recovery with the Four Dimensions," www.ardurecoverycenter.com/support-system-support-a-life-in-recovery-with-the-four-dimensions/#:~:text=The%20four%20dimensions%20are%20a,home%2C%20purpose%2C%20and%20community; Charlotte Johnson, "Four Major Dimensions of Recovery," Care Counseling, www.ardurecoverycenter.com/support-system-support-a-life-in-recovery-with-the-four-dimensions/#:~:text=The%20four%20dimensions%20are%20a,home%2C%20purpose%2C%20and%20community; Amethyst Recovery Center, "Five Factors That Impact Addiction Recovery Success Rates," www.amethystrecovery.org/5-factors-that-impact-addiction-recovery-success-rates/, all accessed October 29, 2023.

3. Ralph Waldo Emerson, *Letters and Social Aims* (Boston: Houghton, 1904), 313.

Session 3

1. Alexander Pope, "An Essay on Man" (London: A. Millar, 1767), 109.

Session 4

1. National Low Income Housing Coalition, "HUD 2022 Annual Homeless Assessment Report Finds Unsheltered Homelessness on the Rise," January 9, 2023, www.nlihc.org/resource/hud-2022-annual-homeless-assessment -report-finds-unsheltered-homelessness-rise.

2. *The Works of Jonathan Edwards*, vol. 1 (London: John Childs, 1839), 426.